M000046736

Digital Photography
POCKET GUIDE

Digital Photography

POCKET GUIDE

Derrick Story

O'REILLY®

Beijing · Cambridge · Farnham · Köln · Paris · Sebastopol · Taipei · Tokyo

Digital Photography Pocket Guide
by Derrick Story

Copyright © 2003 O'Reilly & Associates, Inc. All rights reserved.
Printed in the United States of America.

Published by O'Reilly & Associates, Inc., 1005 Gravenstein Highway North,
Sebastopol, CA 95472.

O'Reilly & Associates books may be purchased for educational,
business, or sales promotional use. Online editions are also available
for most titles (*safari.oreilly.com*). For more information, contact our
corporate/institutional sales department: (800) 998-9938 or
corporate@oreilly.com.

Editors:	Tim O'Reilly and Nancy Kotary
Production Editor:	Colleen Gorman
Cover Designer:	Edie Freedman
Interior Designer:	David Futato

Printing History:

November 2002:	First Edition

Nutshell Handbook, the Nutshell Handbook logo, and the O'Reilly logo
are registered trademarks of O'Reilly & Associates, Inc. Many of the
designations used by manufacturers and sellers to distinguish their
products are claimed as trademarks. Where those designations appear
in this book, and O'Reilly & Associates, Inc. was aware of a trademark
claim, the designations have been printed in caps or initial caps.

While every precaution has been taken in the preparation of this book,
the publisher and author assume no responsibility for errors or
omissions, or for damages resulting from the use of the information
contained herein.

0-596-00454-0
[C]   [3/03]

This book is dedicated to Galen Rowell, who achieved critical acclaim shooting landscape photography with a 35mm camera. By doing so, he opened museum and gallery doors to all small format and digital photographers who want to display the timeless beauty of nature, but prefer to use modern tools instead of traditional large format cameras. Galen and his wife Barbara died in a plane crash on August 11, 2002 in Inyo County, California.

Contents

3. How Do I...

Who's in Charge?

When you first pick up a camera, and hold it in your hands, many thoughts go through your head. Initially, you might wonder where the power button is, or how you turn on the LCD monitor.

Soon, you reach a crossroads with two options before you. The first is to take what you've learned about your camera in the first few minutes, and use that knowledge to take the best pictures you can. Down this path, the camera is merely an acquaintance. It is in charge and does the best it can to help you capture snapshots on vacation or at birthday parties. In return, you try not to drop it and maybe even occasionally clean its lens.

The other path is much different. The first few steps are the steps that everyone takes with a new camera. "How do I make the lens zoom?" "Where's the battery compartment?" But after a short while, you find yourself in territories previously unknown. You begin to wonder, "How can I take a close-up of that flower?" "Can I shoot a portrait at twilight?"

This book is a friendly guide for those who want to take the second path. Down this road, you and your camera will become close friends. You'll get to know every feature and learn how to make outstanding images with them. In a sense, your camera will become an extension of your vision. And that means you're the one making the decisions, not the camera.

Chapter 1: What Is It?

The adventure begins like preparation for any vacation. You have to account for everything that's going to accompany you and know where it is. In Chapter 1, you'll learn about every nook and cranny on your camera. Or, if you haven't purchased one yet, you'll discover the features you need and—just as important—the ones you don't.

Keep your owner's manual handy when you first review Chapter 1. It will help you find where the flash control button is located on your particular model, for instance. Once you find it, this book will show you how to use the different flash modes to take the pictures *you want*, not the ones the camera dictates.

Think of Chapter 1 like a detailed map. It tells you where things are and a little about what they do. It's designed for quick reference—answers while on the road. So make sure you keep this book with you. It's designed to fit easily in your camera bag or your back pocket.

Chapter 2: What Does It Do?

By now, you've located the flash button on your camera, and you've even read about the different modes available, such as *fill flash* and *slow syncho*. Terrific. Now when do you use fill flash? What is slow syncho good for?

Chapter 2 will help you answer those questions. By this time, you're well on your way to becoming close friends with your camera. And you might not notice it, but you've taken control of the situation. In the beginning, the camera made all the decisions. Most of the time they were adequate. Now you're in charge, and your pictures are much better as a result.

Chapter 3: How Do I...

Here you learn 15 important camera techniques. How do you take great outdoor portraits? How can you shoot architecture like a pro? Can you take action shots with a consumer digital camera? Chapter 3 is like an ongoing conversation between two old fishing partners.

By the time you've experimented with the techniques outlined in this pocket reference, you'll have journeyed well beyond others who chose the first path. Soon you'll begin to visualize how the pictures should look in you mind, then be able to make the camera capture those images so you can share them with others. That's what photography is really about—showing others the world as you see it.

The difference between these two paths is *control*. So, who's in charge: you, or the camera?

CHAPTER 1

What Is It?

Digital Camera Components

Camera makers have packed lots of capability into today's compact point-and-shoot models. The camera that you have in your hands, or the one that you're considering buying, probably has more picture-taking ability than you realize. The trick is: how do you discover that hidden potential?

The first steps are to become familiar with your camera's components and understand what they do. This chapter explains important features and sets you on the path to mastering your digital camera.

The chapter is organized by looking at the components on the front, back, top, and sides of the camera. Once you're familiar with the physical buttons and dials, you'll learn about some of the important parts inside, too, such as the image sensor and metering system.

If you're just getting started with digital photography, this section can also help you pick the right model. Each component is rated at one of three levels: *basic*, *intermediate*, or *advanced*. Make a list of the features that best suit your level of photographic experience, then use that list to help you shop. Here's a brief explanation of how each feature is rated in this chapter.

***Basic features* ❶.** These features should be on any digital camera you consider. Avoid a camera that doesn't include all of these components, because odds are you'll be disappointed with its performance.

Intermediate features ❶. In addition to the basics, these features are useful if you have previous photography experience or plan to advance your skill level.

Advanced features Ⓐ. These features are for experienced photographers who are looking for a versatile camera that is capable of producing quality images under a variety of lighting conditions.

If you're interested in a dependable point-and-shoot camera that costs $300 or less, make sure the models you're considering include all the basic features in this section. Mid-level cameras usually run between $300 and $500 and should include most of the intermediate components; more advanced consumer models that run between $500 and $1,000 should have just about every item listed in this section.

Once you buy your camera, spend some time with the owner's manual to become familiar with its unique design and how to use its controls. After that, keep this guide in your camera bag—not only does it provide a quick reference for the major components, but it will also help you understand how to use those features to take better pictures.

Front of the Camera

Figure 1-1 shows the components on the front of an intermediate-level camera. Notice that it includes an optical viewfinder, a focus assist light, and a microphone.

These components are:

Flash Ⓑ. Provides additional light for pictures indoors, at night, or for outdoor portraits.

Focus assist light ❶. Helps your camera focus in dim lighting by projecting a white beam, or a subtle pattern, onto the subject. This light may also shine during red eye reduction flash mode and serve as the warning light when the self timer is activated.

Figure 1-1

The front of an intermediate-level camera

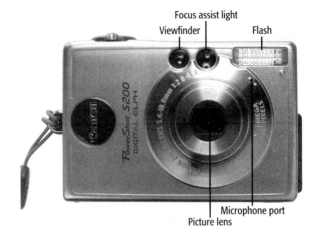

Focus assist light
Viewfinder
Flash

Microphone port
Picture lens

Infrared sensor ⓐ. Primarily used to communicate with the remote control release for cameras that have that capability.

Optical viewfinder lens ⓘ. Lets you compose the picture by looking through the viewfinder lens instead of viewing the LCD monitor on the back of the camera. Using the optical viewfinder saves battery power, but it isn't quite as accurate for framing precise compositions or close-ups.

Microphone port ⓘ. Tiny opening on the front of the camera used to record audio annotations and to add sound to movie clips. Some cameras that have a *movie mode* might have a microphone, but not all do.

Picture-taking lens ⓑⓘⓐ. Projects the image you're shooting on to the electronic sensor where the picture is recorded. This lens also captures the image you see on the LCD monitor on the back of the camera.

Most cameras list a series of numbers on the barrel of the lens or on the body near it. The first set is usually followed by "mm" (which stands for millimeter) and looks something like this:

5.4-10.8 mm or *7-21 mm*

or some other similar combination.

These numbers represent the *zooming range* of your lens. Most consumer digital cameras have a zooming range of 2x or 3x. A 3x zoom lens typically has a more powerful telephoto (to bring the action closer) than a 2x zoom.

A 5.4-10.8mm lens is called a *2x zoom* (multiply 5.4 times two), and a 7-21mm lens is a *3x zoom*. Basic consumer models with a fixed focal length lens (no zoom) will have a single number, such as 7mm.

If you're familiar with 35 mm photography, you can translate those digital camera focal lengths into terms that are easier to understand. A 7-21 mm zoom lens in the digital world is the rough equivalent of a 35-105 mm lens on your traditional SLR.

The second series of numbers usually look something like this:

1:2.8 – 4.0 or *1:2.0 – 2.5*

These numbers represent the *maximum aperture* of the lens at the wide angle and telephoto setting. Aperture determines the amount of light that can pass through the lens to the camera sensor. Wide apertures, such as 2.0 or 2.8, allow a lot of light to pass through the lens, and therefore are better in low-light conditions. More narrow apertures, such as 5.6 or 8, allow less light through the lens and are less desirable for low-light shooting.

Back of the Camera

Figure 1-2 shows the back panel of a basic digital camera. No optical viewfinder is included, so the LCD monitor must always be used for composition. Notice that you change the focal length of the lens by using the two zoom buttons on the back of the camera.

Lens Ratings

Basic ⓑ. Single focal length lens, such as 7mm, with a narrow
maximum aperture such as 5.6 or 8.

Intermediate ⓘ. Short zoom lens (2x) with a maximum aperture
of 2.8 or 4.

Advanced ⓐ. Longer zoom lens (3x) with a maximum aperture of
2.0 or 2.5.

Figure 1-2

Back panel of a basic digital camera

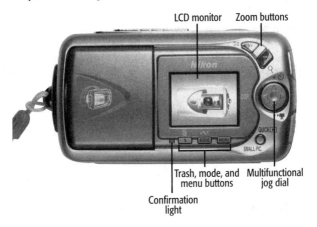

LCD monitor   Zoom buttons

Trash, mode, and   Multifunctional
menu buttons   jog dial

Confirmation
light

Common back panel components include:

Confirmation light ⓑ. Shines when the camera is focused and
ready to fire, or when the flash is ready. Blinking indicator
lights usually suggest that you need to make an adjustment before taking the picture.

Diopter adjustment ⓐ. Allows for manual adjustment of the
optical viewfinder to best suit your vision. This feature is
usually included only on more advanced cameras.

Display on/off button ⑬.   Lets you turn off the display to conserve battery power. Often the button has a third option that provides for the display of camera data on the screen while composing the picture. Typically, you can cycle through these different settings by pushing the button repeatedly.

Jog dial ⑩.   Enables you to navigate through on-screen menus by pressing the four directional buttons. Sometimes jog dial buttons have two sets of functions: one set for changing settings while in picture-taking mode, and the other for making adjustments in picture-viewing mode. Look for little icons next to the jog dial buttons. They usually represent the functions associated with those buttons in picture taking mode.

LCD monitor ⑧.   Allows for precise framing of the subject, because the image is captured directly through the picture-taking lens. You should always use the LCD monitor in macro mode (for close-ups) or when using the digital zoom function. The LCD monitor is also used for reviewing pictures you've already captured. Most LCD monitors, however, aren't effective in direct sunlight. The image is hard to see. If you shoot lots of outdoor pictures, make sure you have an optical viewfinder as well.

Menu button ⑨.   Activates the on-screen menu that enables you to set the various functions of the camera. Most likely, you'll use the multifunctional jog dial to navigate through those menus.

Mode switch ⑥.   Allows you to switch between picture taking and picture reviewing modes. If your camera allows you to shoot short movies, that will be a third position of this switch.

Optical viewfinder ①.   Lets you compose the picture by looking through a separate viewfinder lens instead of the LCD monitor on the back of the camera. Using the optical viewfinder saves battery power, but it isn't quite as accurate for framing precise compositions or close-ups. The optical viewfinder is very useful when shooting outdoors in direct sunlight, because LCD monitors don't fare well under these conditions and are difficult to see.

Figure 1-3 displays components on the back of an intermediate-level camera. An optical viewfinder is included in addition to the LCD monitor. Notice the icons associated with each button on the multifunctional jog dial: these represent features you can activate in *picture taking* mode.

Figure 1-3

The back of an intermediate camera

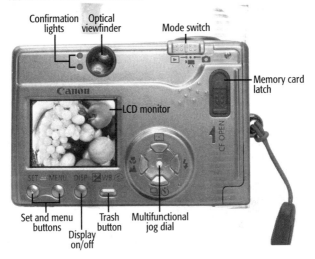

These additional features include:

Set or confirmation button ⓐ. Press this to confirm a choice. Most cameras insist that you confirm all selections before enabling them. This is particularly important when erasing pictures so you don't accidentally delete a picture by inadvertently pressing the erase button.

Trash button **⓫.** Removes the current picture displayed on the LCD monitor. This button doesn't usually remove all pictures on a memory card; you have to select the "erase all" function via the onscreen menu.

Top of Camera

The top deck of a compact camera (as shown in Figure 1-4) has fewer controls than more advanced models. This Canon uses a "ring type" zoom lever around the shutter to adjust the focal length.

Figure 1-4

The top of a compact camera

Features frequently located on the top of a camera include:

LCD information screen **⓭.** Displays camera information, such as number of pictures remaining on the memory card, exposure compensation setting, and flash mode. This screen is particularly handy when you're using the optical viewfinder to compose your pictures with the LCD monitor turned off. Most advanced cameras include a LCD information screen on the top deck.

Hot shoe 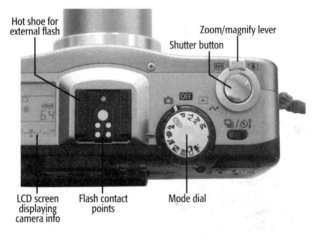. Provides a connection for external flash and other camera accessories. The metal contacts allow the camera to communicate with the flash to provide advanced features such as dedicated exposure control.

Figure 1-5 shows the top of a more advanced digital camera. Note the standard hot shoe for mounting a dedicated flash and the LCD screen with camera data. The mode dial includes a variety of settings, including aperture priority, manual mode, and programmed exposure.

Figure 1-5

Top view of an advanced consumer digital camera

Hot shoe for external flash

Zoom/magnify lever

Shutter button

LCD screen displaying camera info

Flash contact points

Mode dial

Features shown include:

Mode dial . Allows you to select the picture taking mode, such as programmed exposure, aperture priority, or manual.

Shutter button ❽. Trips the shutter, yes, but also provides focus and exposure lock. For the best pictures, press lightly on the shutter button and hold it in the halfway position to lock the focus and exposure. Once the confirmation light comes on, you're ready to take the picture. Then add more pressure until the shutter trips. The trick is not to let up on the shutter button once the focus is locked, but to keep the pressure on in the halfway position until the exposure is made. Almost all digital cameras use this type of two-step shutter button.

Zoom/magnify lever ❾. Use this lever to zoom in and out when composing your image in picture-taking mode. When in picture review mode, this lever also allows you to magnify your image on the LCD monitor for closer inspection.

Bottom and Sides of the Camera

Figure 1-6 shows the bottom view of a digital camera, including the tripod socket.

Figure 1-6

Bottom view of camera

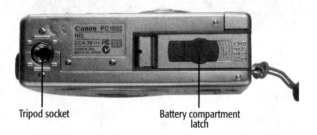

Tripod socket

Battery compartment latch

Additional features around the rest of the camera include:

Camera strap ❾. Secures the camera by allowing you to place a strap around your wrist or neck. Most compact cameras use the wrist-style strap.

Computer connection ❽. Used for transferring pictures from camera to computer. Most cameras provide a USB (Universal Serial Bus) cable to make this connection.

Remote release ❹. Provides for firing of camera from distances up to 15 feet. Some remote releases also allow you to operate the zoom lens. For best results, point the sensor on the remote release at the infrared sensor on the front of the camera.

Speaker port ❹. Emits audio playback of digital video or verbal annotations—designed primarily for quick review on location. For best listening quality, upload the data to your computer and use its sound system for playback.

Tripod socket ❾. Attaches the camera to a tripod or flash bracket. Metal sockets are more durable and therefore superior to plastic ones.

Inside the Camera

In this section, you'll learn the common features of digital cameras' innards, starting with how the unit is powered. Figure 1-7 shows the camera loaded with alkaline batteries that are often included in the box. In the long run, you're much better off switching to rechargeable NiMH batteries such as shown in the figure.

Battery ❽

The battery provides the power for camera functions. This is one feature that every digital camera must have. Common battery types are alkaline, lithium-ion, and nickel-metal hydride—the latter two are rechargeable.

Figure 1-7

Two different types of batteries: alkaline and NiMH

If your camera came with alkaline AA batteries, use them for testing, then replace them as soon as possible with rechargeable nickel-metal hydride (NiMH) batteries, which last much longer than alkalines and will save you lots of money over the long haul, because you can recharge and reuse them. It's always good, however, to keep a fresh set of alkalines handy in case your NiMHs run out of juice while you're away from your charger. Another good practice is to have two sets of the rechargeables, so one's always ready to use—they're a little expensive, but still much cheaper than buying new alkalines over and over.

Lithium-ions are very popular with major camera makers such as Sony, Nikon, and Canon. Most of these cameras come with their own proprietary battery and its matching charger. Lithium-ions typically have great capacity and hold their charge for a long time, but you might want to buy an extra battery since you can't use readily available alkalines as a back up.

Exposure Meter ⓑⓘⓐ

The meter reads the light passing through the lens and determines the proper shutter speed and aperture to produce a well-exposed picture.

All digital cameras have some type of exposure meter, but many models have more than one *pattern* for measuring light. The three most common patterns are: *center-weighted*, *evaluative*, and *spot*. Advanced cameras may include all three of these metering patterns, while more basic models may rely on center-weighted or evaluative:

Center-weighted ⓑ.   The entire picture area is measured by the meter, with extra emphasis placed on subjects in the center of the frame.

Evaluative ⓘ.   The image area is divided into sections (usually six or more), and light is measured in each section. The camera then "evaluates" each section and matches the overall pattern to data stored in its computer system. The resulting camera settings are determined by how the pattern and data match up.

Spot ⓘ.   Only the center area of the viewing area, usually indicated by brackets, measures light to determine the exposure. Spot metering is helpful in contrast lighting situations that might fool other metering patterns.

Image Sensor ⓑⓘⓐ

Converts light energy passing through the camera lens into a digital signal. The most common sensors are CCDs, which stands for Charged-Coupled Device. Some cameras are now using CMOS (Complementary Metal Oxide Semiconductor) sensors that share many of the same attributes with CCD types, but use less energy.

Once again, what matters is the size of the sensor, or more specifically, how many *pixels* (picture elements) it supports. Today's cameras sensors support millions of pixels, and the term *megapixel* means just that: a million pixels. So instead of saying, "I just bought a camera has a sensor that supports 2,000,000 pixels," you say, "I just bought a two-megapixel camera."

Consumer cameras range in capacity from 1.3 to 6 megapixels. Generally speaking, you want at least 2 megapixels for snap shooting and vacation pictures. The more megapixels your camera has, the bigger the prints you can make. Two-megapixel cameras can produce photo-quality prints up to 5 × 7"; 3-megapixel models are good up to 8 × 10"; and 4-megapixel advanced digicams can produce very nice 11 × 14" prints.

If your main goal is to produce pictures to send via email or for posting on your web site, cameras in the 1.3 megapixel range ❶ should be fine. But if you like to make prints of your digital images, see this table for your ideal camera.

Camera type	Photo quality	Acceptable
2MP ❶	5 × 7	8 × 10
3MP ❶	8 × 10	11 × 14
4MP ❷	11 × 14	12 × 16
5MP ❷	12 × 16	16 × 20

Memory Cards ❸

Memory cards store picture data on an electronic card that's inserted into the camera body. Nearly every digital camera contains some type of removable memory. When the camera takes a picture and creates the data for that image, it "writes" that information on the memory card. This enables you to retrieve or transfer your electronic pictures long after they've been recorded.

The most popular type of card is CompactFlash (CF), but SmartMedia (SM), Sony Memory Stick (MS), IBM MicroDrive,

MultimediaCard (MMC), Secure Digital (SD), and the latest entry, xD-Picture Card introduced by Fuji and Olympus, are also capable alternatives.

Figure 1-8 shows an Olympus camera with its SmartMedia memory card. Even though it comes with a 16MB card, that's not nearly enough capacity for this 3-megapixel camera—a 64 or 128MB card makes more sense.

Figure 1-8

Olympus camera with SmartMedia memory card

Figure 1-9 shows a Nikon with CompactFlash memory card: most Nikon and Canon models use these CompactFlash memory cards, which are sold in many locations and easy on the pocketbook.

The type of memory card your digicam accepts isn't as important as the size of card you're using. Most cameras ship with *starter memory cards* that hold only 8 or 16MB. These are fine during the learning phase, but once you're ready to take your camera on vacation or photograph your daughter's birthday party, you'll need much more capacity.

Figure 1-9

CompactFlash

This handy table will help you determine the best capacity for your camera.

Camera type (megapixels)	Minimum card (megabytes)	Recommended card (megabytes)
2MP	32MB	64MB
3MP	64MB	128MB
4MP	128MB	256MB

Other storage features include:

Mass storage USB ❶. Enables the camera to be connected to a computer without using any special drivers, much in the same way an external hard drive is mounted by plugging it in. You can then "drag and drop" your pictures from the camera to the computer or use a image application to download them.

Digital cameras that are USB Mass Storage devices can be connected to computers running the following operating systems without installing any software: Windows XP, 2000, and ME, plus Macintosh 9.x and Mac OS X 10.1 or later.

RAM buffer ❶. Stores image data in the camera's Random Access Memory before transferring it to the memory card. The RAM buffer enables advanced functionality, such as burst and movie modes. The camera can move picture data to the RAM buffer much faster than writing it to the memory card. So when you use burst mode, for example, the camera captures a sequence of shots in the RAM buffer, then transfers the data to the memory card after you've released the shutter button. RAM buffers can be as large as 32 megabytes. The larger the buffer, the longer your shot sequences can be.

Self timer ❶. Delays the shutter release for approximately 10 seconds. Activating the self timer is an easy way for the photographer to join a group shot. Sometimes this function is used instead of a remote release to trip the shutter without jarring the camera. This is especially useful in low light situations with slow shutter speeds when the camera is mounted on a tripod.

Video out connection ❶. Allows you to connect the camera directly to a television or other monitor to display pictures on a larger screen. Using video out is an easy way to show your pictures to a large group of people.

Putting It All Together

Now that you're familiar with the features of your digital camera, how do you use them to take great pictures? In the next chapter, *What Does It Do?*, you'll learn helpful techniques such as how to master the focus lock feature of your shutter button, choose the right flash setting for different types of lighting situations, and carefully inspect your pictures *before* uploading them to your computer—plus lots more. Great pictures are only a chapter away.

CHAPTER 2

What Does It Do?
The Digital Photographer's Toolbox

Now that you're familiar with your camera's basic components, you can concentrate on how to unlock their picture taking magic. For example, a simple flash menu button ($\frac{1}{2}$) allows you to cycle through a series of versatile lighting controls. But what do the controls mean, and which one should you choose?

In this chapter, you'll learn how to use those seemingly simple buttons and dials to tap the incredible picture-taking capacity of your digital camera.

Taking Control of Buttons, Dials, and Menus

This section covers camera controls alphabetically from A to Z, or more specifically, from Aperture Priority to Zooming. New terms are listed in *italic*. If you're not sure where to find any of these settings on your particular camera, double check the owner's manual, or refer to Chapter 1 of this guide.

It's best to have your camera in hand as you work with the text and study the photo examples. The more you shoot, the more natural these techniques will become.

Aperture Priority Mode (AV)

Many intermediate and advanced cameras allow you to choose the aperture setting, and the camera sets the proper corresponding shutter speed. This setting is sometimes denoted as *AV*, which stands for *aperture value*. Typically, you can access this setting on your camera via the Mode Dial, or sometimes as a menu option.

Choose the aperture priority mode when you want to control the *depth of field*. In other words, how much of your picture, from front to back, do you want in focus? Shallow depth-of-field is often used for portraits—your subject is in focus, but everything else is a little soft. Choose an aperture value of 2.0, 2.8, or 4 for this type of shooting situation. The lower the value, the shallower the depth of field and less of the image will be in focus (see Table 2-1 for specific depth-of-field settings).

Table 2-1. Depth-of-field settings

f-stop	Diameter of aperture	Depth-of-field	Background looks
f-2	Very large diameter	Very shallow	Very soft
f-2.8	Large diameter	Shallow	Soft
f-4	Medium diameter	Moderate	A little out of focus
f-5.6	Medium diameter	Moderate	A little out of focus
f-8	Small diameter	Moderately deep	Mostly in focus
f-11	Small diameter	Deep	Sharp
f-16	Very small diameter	Very deep	Very sharp

When shooting landscapes, you will probably want "deep" depth-of-field, which produces a sharp image from foreground to background. You should choose an aperture value of 8, 11, or 16 for deeper depth-of-field.

Shooting an outdoor portrait with a soft background

See Figure 2-1 for an example. If your camera has a portrait-shooting mode, it's designed to "open up" the aperture to provide a shallow depth of field. Or, you can use aperture priority and select f-2, f-2.5, or f-2.8. Place the subject at least 10 feet away from the background, more if possible. This will soften the background detail, putting more emphasis on your subject. Set your zoom lens to the telephoto position (this enhances the soft background effect even more). Focus on the model's eyes. Press the shutter halfway to "lock" the focus. While still holding the shutter in the halfway position, recompose so the composition is just the way you want it. Then take the picture. If the lighting on the model's face isn't to your liking, force the flash on (see the entry for "Flash Modes" later in this chapter), and shoot again. This setup should provide a nicely focused model against a softened background.

Figure 2-1

Soft background portrait: lens zoomed to telephoto position and aperture set wide open to limit depth of field. Fill flash added.

Auto Exposure

See *Programmed Exposure*.

Burst/Continuous Shooting Mode

All but the most basic cameras have some sort of *burst* or *continuous shooting* mode (indicated by layers of rectangles). Typically this mode is a menu option, but some cameras display it as a button option that you can access directly while in picture taking mode. Either way, it allows you to shoot a series of pictures while holding the shutter button in the down position—see Figure 2-2. The number of pictures you can record in one burst is determined by the capacity of your camera's *RAM buffer*.

Most people use this continuous shooting feature for recording sports events. And it is a great choice for capturing a baseball player's swing or a quarterback's touchdown pass. But burst modes can also help you compensate for *shutter lag*—that diabolical delay from the moment you press the shutter to when the picture is actually recorded. Some digital cameras have shutter lags as long as a second or two, which is a lifetime in action photography.

Figure 2-2

Burst mode—short series was taken with continuous mode on, flash off, in programmed auto mode (f-4.5 @ 1/640th of a second)

Capturing the Decisive Moment

To catch the precise moment that your son blows out the candles on his fifth birthday, set your camera to *continuous* or *burst* mode. Make sure the activity is in a well-lit room or even better, outdoors (and turn your flash off—flashes can't fire fast enough to keep pace with burst modes). Focus on the child and hold the shutter down half way to "lock it in." Still holding the shutter in the halfway position, recompose. Start the series as he prepares to blow out the candles and shoot continuously until the RAM buffer fills up and the camera stops taking pictures. You'll have to wait a moment for the camera to process all the information you've just recorded. Then go back through the sequence and choose the picture that best depicts the decisive moment. You can either erase the others to save memory card space, or keep them to show the entire sequence.

Close-Up Mode

Digital cameras are great for getting in real tight with your subject. This is sometimes referred to as *macro photography*. Unlike most film cameras, digicams usually have the macro capability built right into the camera—you don't need any special accessories for impressive close-ups. Usually, you can access the macro mode by pressing the button that has the "flower" icon next to it. Some cameras bury this option in the onscreen menu and force you to dig a little bit to find it.

The main thing to remember with close-up photography is that whenever you increase lens magnification, you have to hold the camera extra steady to prevent camera shake, which can make your picture look out of focus due to too much camera movement during the exposure. For important close-ups that you plan on printing, you may even want to steady the camera using a tripod. The rule of thumb is that *increased magnification means increased camera shake*.

Also, your depth of field is very shallow in close up photography, so be sure to focus on the element that is most important to you. If you have an aperture priority mode, you can increase the depth of field a little more by using the f-11 or f-16 setting. The higher the number for the f-stop setting, the more depth of field you'll have. See Figure 2-3.

Figure 2-3

Recorded in close-up mode with the spot meter on, flash off, and in aperture priority mode set to 5.6

PRACTICAL EXAMPLE

Taking a Close Up of a Flower

Put your camera on a tripod. Turn on the close-up mode, and turn off your flash (many digital camera flashes overexpose subjects at very close range). Focus your camera on the most important element in the composition and hold the shutter halfway down to lock in the focus. While still holding the shutter in the halfway position, recompose if you need to, then shoot the picture. If there's a breeze blowing, wait for a calm moment before shooting: your picture will be sharper. Review your work after a few shots, then make any necessary adjustments. If you have a manual focus option on your camera, you can compose your picture first, then manually focus. Use the self-timer or the remote release to trip the shutter—that will prevent you from jarring the camera when you take the shot.

Composition

Whether you're using the LCD monitor or the optical viewfinder, the composition of your picture determines a large part of its success. *Composition* is the arrangement of the elements in your photograph. The subject, the horizon line, background elements—they all play a role in the successful composition. And this is just as true with the most basic of point-and-shoot cameras as it is with a top-of-the-line Nikon digital SLR.

The first step to creating great photographs is to consider all elements in your viewfinder. Here are a few questions to ask yourself when framing your picture: Where is the subject placed? Are there any distracting background elements, such as telephone poles? Is the horizon line straight? Should you raise the camera angle or lower it?

Most photographers keep five rules of thumb in mind when composing their shots. These are not hard and fast rules, but they are worth remembering and applying as often as possible.

Get closer.   Use your feet and your zoom lens to frame your subject as tightly as possible. Once you get closer and compose your image, take a few shots, then get closer again. Your pictures will improve dramatically.

Remember the Rule of Thirds.   Don't always put your subject dead center in the frame. Instead, divide the frame into thirds and position the important elements along those lines. Your compositions will be less static and more interesting.

Eliminate busy backgrounds.   Trees are great, but not growing out of the tops of people's heads. Look out for busy patterns, bright objects, and other distracting elements.

Go high, go low.   Change your camera angle when working a shot. Get low on the ground and shoot upward. Raise the camera over your head and shoot down—swiveling lens and LCD monitors make this easier than ever.

Simple is better.   Try not to clutter your compositions with nonessential elements. Keep things simple, move in close, and find an interesting arrangement.

A Simple but Powerful Landscape

Look for a situation where you can create an interesting picture with just a few elements. In Figure 2-4, the composition includes sky, water, mountains, and a thin strip of land. The most powerful element is the sky, so the photographer used a polarizing filter to add drama, then composed to let it occupy 70 percent of the frame. Too often, people will split the frame in half between sky and land resulting in a far less interesting and dynamic image. Also notice how the horizon line is straight across the frame. This is very important or the picture will "feel" wrong. Finally, the photographer waited until the shadows from the clouds moved into position to enhance the composition. This creates a layering of lights and darks: a technique used by master landscape photographers for years. Seemingly simple at first view, this composition employs many important techniques.

Figure 2-4

Simple composition: captured using the evaluative metering pattern and auto-program mode

Compression or Image Quality

Another way in which digital cameras are much different than their film counterparts is that they actually let you set the *quality of the image* via the *compression* or *image quality* setting. All digital cameras save images as some form of JPEG (Joint Photographic Experts Group) file. If you've worked with JPEGs, you know that you can save them at various quality levels, usually from 1 to 10. A JPEG saved at level 1 has very poor quality and a very small file size—it is said to be *highly compressed*. The same file saved at level 10 has excellent image quality but the corresponding file size is quite large—it is *minimally compressed*.

Your digital camera gives you some of these same options in the compression or image quality setting, which is usually one of the first items you'll see when you open the onscreen menu. Instead of providing you with number values such as "3," "6," and "9," cameras use terms such as *basic*, *normal*, and *fine*; or *normal*, *fine*, and *superfine*. Regardless of the actual terms used, pay attention to the order they are listed.

Basic or *normal* is low resolution and should be avoided, because it limits your ability to make good prints. Don't be tempted by the number of extra pictures you can squeeze on a card using low resolution—it is much better to buy a bigger memory card instead.

Normal or *fine* is medium resolution and is acceptable for emailing pictures or images for the Web. You can also make decent prints from images at this setting.

Fine or *superfine* is the highest resolution setting on your camera and the one you should consider using all the time. True, you can't get as many pictures squeezed on to your memory card as the other lower resolution settings, but you're capturing images at their highest quality and you always have the potential of producing quality prints or large web images from all of your shots.

Some cameras also provide a *raw* or *Tiff* resolution setting. These settings don't use any compression and produce very large file sizes. If you know that the final product is going to be a large print or a picture in a magazine, then these settings are worth considering. But for everyday shooting, they might be overkill.

For general shooting, you should be happy with the quality of pictures set at the lowest compressed level, which is usually *fine* or *superfine*. Figure 2-5 illustrates compression-level settings.

Figure 2-5

Compression levels: in this menu the "S" stands for "Superfine," which is this camera's highest quality setting

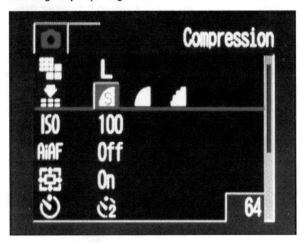

Continuous Shooting Mode

See *Burst/Continuous Shooting Mode*.

Deleting Images

See *Erasing Images*.

Digital Zoom

Unlike the *optical zoom* on your camera, which consists of actual glass elements, the *digital zoom* is a function of the camera's electronics. By enabling the digital zoom, you can increase the magnification of your lens to bring your subjects even closer than is possible with just the optics alone.

For example, if your optical zoom is 3X (7mm to 21mm focal length) and your digital zoom adds another 3X, then you have the equivalent of a 7mm to 42mm lens.

The tradeoff is that you compromise image quality when you use the digital zoom. Since it's a function of the camera's electronics and not the actual lens, the digital zoom is really emulating the telephoto effect instead of actually recording the image. Even though you "get closer" using the digital zoom, there's some quality loss too.

Avoid using the digital zoom for normal, everyday shooting. But when you encounter situations where getting the shot is more important than a little quality loss, the digital zoom can be a very helpful tool. See Figure 2-6 for an example.

Erasing Images

There are two types of erasing. Most photographers use the *single erase* option when they take a bad picture and want to get rid of it to free up space on the memory card. Cameras usually have a "trash" button for this procedure. The other type of erasing is the *Erase All* command, which wipes every picture off your card, usually after you've just uploaded them to your computer. Most often the Erase All command is a menu item. You can use the *Format Card* command, too. You should be careful with both. Double-check that you have indeed uploaded your pictures to your computer before wiping clean the memory card.

As for single erase: sometimes photographers discard images too quickly before fully examining them. Obviously some pictures need to go right away: you're in a dark room and the flash doesn't fire; it's a pretty safe bet to dump that shot. But if you take a series of images and want to erase all but the best, then make sure you carefully examine the others. Many digital cameras provide a magnify function for the LCD monitor. Try zooming in on your potential discards and examine them closely before pressing the trash button. To be extra safe, view them on the computer, then trash them if they still don't make the cut. You can miss subtle details viewing pictures on the tiny LCD monitor, and sometimes those very details make a great shot.

Exposure Compensation

One of the most valuable tools available on your digital camera is the *exposure compensation* scale, which allows you to override your camera's auto exposure reading so you can capture the image exactly the way you want it. On some cameras, this is a button option that you can get to easily, and on others it's a menu item that's not quite as convenient. Either way, you might want to find exposure compensation on your camera, because it can help you take better pictures.

Figure 2-6

Optical versus digital zoom: top image captured with the camera's optical zoom set to 3X; bottom image taken from the same position with the digital zoom enabled adding another 3.7X for an effective zoom range of 6.7X

Doesn't your camera always know the right exposure to set? Unfortunately not. The light meter in your camera is calibrated to expose properly for anything that's 18 percent gray. This represents the approximate light reflection of a deep blue sky or green foliage, which is the most common background in outdoor shots (or at least used to be when camera meters were first calibrated). And indeed, your light meter works great most of the time.

But what if you want to shoot a white picket fence on a bright day? It's not 18 percent gray; it's white! If you don't override your camera's light meter via exposure compensation, then guess what shade your camera will render that white fence—18 percent gray. In effect, your automatic wonder digicam has *underexposed* the white fence (Figure 2-7).

Figure 2-7

Underexposed fence

You can use your camera's exposure compensation option to render the image correctly. When you find the control, you'll see a scale with "0" in the middle, "plus" numbers to the right, and "negative" numbers to the left. Figure 2-8 shows the fence again.

Figure 2-8

Properly exposed fence: exposure compensation control set to +1

When you're shooting an object that's very bright, such as the picket fence, you want to *add* more exposure to render it white. So move the pointer on the exposure scale to +1 (see Figure 2-9).

Figure 2-9

Exposure compensation scale

$$-2 \quad . \quad . \quad 1 \quad . \quad . \quad 0 \quad . \quad . \quad +1 \quad . \quad . \quad +2$$

If, on the other hand, you are shooting a very dark object in auto-exposure mode, the camera tends to overexpose the shot and render the object lighter than it really is. In this situation, you should subtract exposure by moving the pointer on the exposure scale to –1. See Figures 2-10 and 2-11 for examples.

As you become more comfortable using the exposure compensation function, you can make more subtle adjustments to your pictures. You can also fine-tune your images later in Photoshop or some other editor, but the more accurately you capture your pictures in the first place, the less time you'll have to spend processing them later.

Figure 2-10

Overexposed dark objects

Exposure Lock

Typically, when you press the shutter button halfway and hold it there, the camera locks in both the *focus* and the *exposure*. While still holding the button halfway down, you can then recompose the shot and take the picture. But you might want to lock the focus on one item and the exposure on another element.

Some cameras allow you to *lock* the exposure independently of the focus. If your camera has this function, it usually works like this: first, you press the shutter button halfway to take a meter reading; while still holding the shutter button down, you press another button to lock in the exposure. An indicator usually appears on the LCD screen to let you know you've locked the exposure. Now you can focus on another element and take the picture. Remember to turn off the exposure lock once you're done working that particular shot.

Figure 2-11

Properly exposed dark objects: exposure compensation pointer set to -1

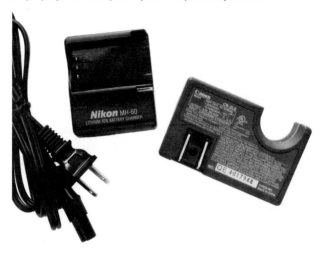

You can use exposure lock as a shortcut for exposure compensation. Instead of accessing the exposure scale and adjusting your image that way, you can find a middle tone in the picture you want to shoot, such as a patch of grass, and lock your exposure on it. This is a faster way to override your camera's auto exposure setting in difficult lighting situations.

Exposure Metering

Most digital cameras rely on *programmed auto exposure* metering to set the aperture and shutter speed. Essentially, the camera's light meter "reads" the light and compares the data to a set of instructions stored in the camera's memory. The camera then chooses the best aperture/shutter speed combination based on the data it receives from the light meter.

The most important thing you need to know about exposure metering is that cameras are not perfect when it comes to evaluating exposure. They are most often fooled when presented with very bright or very dark subjects.

Fortunately, most cameras allow you to override the programmed exposure setting. See the entry for *Exposure Compensation*.

File Format

JPEG (Joint Photographic Experts Group) is the format used by most digital cameras. JPEG files are very portable and can be read by nearly every computer and web browser. JPEG files use compression to keep the file size small for easy transport. Users can determine the amount of compression by selection options from the menu function on their digital cameras—usually "high," "medium," and "low," but not always using those exact terms. For example, the terms "Superfine," "Fine," and "Normal" are used by Canon. See the *Compression or Image Quality* entry for more detail about these settings.

Over the last few years, a specialized version of JPEG has emerged for digital camera use. EXIF (Exchangeable Image File) has the same compression properties as standard JPEGs, but allows the camera to record additional data to the picture file—such as shutter speed, aperture, date, etc.—that can be "read" by most modern image editors. This additional information is sometimes referred to as *metadata*, and it's a real blessing for photographers who like access to the technical specs for every shot they record, but hate taking notes. The current EXIF version is 2.1.

TIFFs (Tagged Image File Format) are sometimes available as an alternate "high quality" format. As used on digital cameras, TIFFs are not usually compressed, so file sizes are very large. For general shooting, using the "high quality" JPEG setting is just fine. But for those special situations when you want to squeeze every drop of quality from the image, the TIFF setting might be appropriate.

Some camera makers also provide a "raw" format option that is also uncompressed. As with TIFFs, the file sizes are large, and the quality is very high.

Film Speed

See *ISO Speed*.

Flash Compensation

This feature enables you to manually adjust the flash exposure, and is more common on advanced cameras than basic point-and-shoots.

Much in the same way that *exposure compensation* gives you a tool for fine tuning your camera's programmed auto exposure, flash compensation provides a way to increase or decrease light output. So if your subject is too bright after you take a test shot (overexposed), you can set flash compensation to -1 to decrease output. On the other hand, if your model is rendered too dark after taking the first shot, you can set flash compensation to +1 to increase light output.

Flash Modes   ⚡

The default flash mode for most cameras is automatic, and that's where it stays for most folks. But even the most basic digicams offer multiple flash settings that can help you take engaging photos under a variety of lighting conditions. Some of the typical flash settings that you might encounter on your camera are:

Auto. The camera activates the flash as determined by the light meter reading. If you're indoors in low light, the flash fires. Outside on a bright sunny day? The camera turns the flash off.

Red eye reduction. Many digicams have some sort of red eye reduction mode. Red eye occurs when the subject's eyes are dilated (in dim lighting), exposing the retina. When the light from the flash reflects off the retina, the result is red eye. Most cameras tackle this problem by shining a light at the subject before the flash goes off. The thinking is that this preflash will cause the pupils to constrict and reduce the chance for red eye.

The challenge for the photographer using red eye reduction flash modes is coping with the extended delay from the time the shutter button is pressed until the actual picture is recorded. If you use red eye reduction, remind the subject to hold the pose until the final flash has fired. And remember to hold the camera steady during this entire process.

Auto red eye reduction. The combination of *auto* and *red eye reduction* modes. The camera uses red eye reduction whenever it determines that flash is required.

Flash on. This setting is usually referred to as *fill flash*. The camera will fire the flash with every exposure regardless of the light meter reading. *Flash on* is one of the most useful camera settings, because it allows you to take professional-looking portraits outdoors by adding enough light to properly illuminate the subject while balancing the exposure for the background. The result is a beautiful image with all components properly exposed.

Flash off. Sometimes the flash destroys the mood of a shot. This is particularly true with indoor portraits where the subject is next to a window with daylight streaming in. Creative photographers like to turn off the flash in these settings, steady the camera, and record an *existing light* photograph that renders a more artistic picture.

Slow-synchro flash. Often referred to as *nighttime* mode, this setting tells your camera to use a slow shutter speed in combination with the flash. By doing this, you can capture more background detail in dimly lit scenes such as portraits shot at twilight or indoor shooting where you want to capture the mood of the setting, in addition to having your main subject properly exposed by the flash. Remember to hold the camera very steady when using *slow-synchro flash* to prevent blurring of the background. If you have a tripod, you may want to use it for these types of shots.

PRACTICAL EXAMPLE

Exciting Nighttime Portraits

If you're in New York City at night, you don't want the background to go completely black for your portraits because your shots would be missing half the fun. (You could be in New Jersey for all anyone knows.) To capture the vibrancy of the city, set your camera to *slow-synchro* or *nighttime flash mode*. Some cameras, such as the Canon PowerShot S230 and the Nikon Coolpix 3500, hide this setting unless you enable the *manual mode*. Check your camera's user guide if you can't find this flash setting. Once you have slow-synchro flash turned on, you camera will do its best to balance the low light background with the flash exposure of your main subject.

Figure 2-12 illustrates slow-synchro flash mode. This image in Times Square, NYC, was captured using the slow-synchro flash mode. By choosing this setting, the camera selected a shutter speed slow enough to capture the background information while adding enough light from the flash to illuminate the main subject. (Settings were 1/10th of a second at f-3.2. Canon PowerShot S200 in slow-synchro mode.)

The trick to getting great shots using this technique is to remember to hold the camera very steady until it's done recording the scene; otherwise, you might end up with a blurry background. Sometimes it's useful to mount the camera on a tripod, but if you don't have one available, you can set it on a solid surface and use the *self-timer* to trip the shutter, increasing your odds of capturing a well-lit, sharp background to complement your main subject.

Figure 2-12

Slow-synchro flash

Focus Lock

One of the most common pitfalls with point-and-shoot cameras is their tendency to focus on the object in the center of the viewfinder—whether or not it's the intended subject. Instead of capturing your best friend perfectly exposed and in focus, the back wall 10 feet away is sharp as a tack and your buddy is a fuzzy blob in the foreground. The odds for this scenario are particularly high if your buddy is standing off to one side of the frame or the other.

You can prevent the blurring of your subject by using focus lock. Simply point your camera directly at the primary subject, then press the shutter button down halfway until the focus confirmation light goes on. Continue holding the shutter button down in the halfway position and recompose your shot. Then take the picture.

Two-Person Portraits

Focus lock is especially important when taking pictures of two people. For example, your kids are having a good time at the playground and you want to capture the moment. You ask them to turn toward the camera and you fire off a quick shot. Upon review, you see that the swing set in the background is perfectly focused, but your boys are not (Figure 2-13).

That's because if your camera has a single focusing sensor, it will almost always be positioned directly between your subjects on a two-person portrait. The solution is to lock the focus on one person, recompose, then take the shot (Figure 2-14).

Figure 2-13

Main subjects out of focus

Figure 2-14

Subjects in focus, after locking the focus and recomposing the shot

Format Memory Card

Often included as a menu item, *Format Memory Card* is an alternative to *Erase All Pictures*. Either procedure clears your memory card of all images so you can shoot more pictures, but Format Memory Card also customizes the memory card to your camera by writing a small amount of data to it. This is a good option to choose before you start using a new memory card, or if you're switching memory cards from another camera.

Infinity Lock

Some cameras have an *infinity setting* that allows you to "lock" the focus on subjects that are 10 feet away or farther. At first this might not seem like an overly useful addition to your camera's feature set, but infinity lock is particularly handy in situations when you camera's auto focus system has difficulty "locking in" on a subject, causing it to "hunt" as it searches for the correct setting. In this case, you simply select the infinity lock and shoot away.

Infinity lock helps reduce *shutter lag* too. If, for example, you're taking pictures at your daughter's soccer game and are missing too many shots because of the lag between the time you press the shutter button and the moment the picture is actually recorded, then try the infinity lock. The camera is now pre-focused and will respond more quickly.

If you're shooting landscapes through a car or train window and the camera is having a hard time focusing through the glass, then enabling the infinity lock feature should solve your problem.

ISO Speed

Sometimes referred to as "film speed," *ISO speed* is actually a better term for expressing the light sensitivity of your digital camera. ISO stands for International Organization for Standardization. This entity has established many standards, including the light sensitivity of photographic materials.

If your camera has multiple ISO speed settings, then you can use these adjustments to increase the light sensitivity of the image sensor. The default setting for most digicams is *ISO 100*. This is the speed setting for general photography. If you're in a low-light situation and need to increase the sensitivity of you image sensor, change the ISO Speed setting from 100 to 200, or even 400, if necessary. Each setting is the equivalent to one f-stop of light.

Keep in mind though, that increasing the ISO speed also increases *image noise*, which decrease the quality of your picture. Sometimes this tradeoff is worth it, but for everyday shooting, make sure your ISO Speed setting is 100 or lower.

Important reminder! If you do increase the ISO speed for a special situation, be sure to change the setting back to 100 right after the shoot. You will be sorely disappointed if you photograph a beautiful landscape the next day at ISO 400.

JPEG

See *File Format*.

Macro Mode

See *Close-Up Mode.*

Magnify Control

See *Zoom/Magnify Control.*

Manual Exposure Setting

Many digital cameras allow only programmed auto exposure, but more advanced models also provide complete control over the aperture and speed settings. If your camera has this option, it's probably denoted as *Manual*, or *Manual Exposure*.

In traditional film photography, switching to *manual mode* was the true test of manhood. The photographer would fiddle with the aperture and shutter speed settings, then hope that the pictures were properly exposed when they returned from the photo finisher. This process was by no means for the faint of heart.

But digital photography has changed all of that, and manual mode is much more friendly, because you can preview the final result on the LCD monitor before you press the shutter button. Now manual mode represents both control and convenience.

For outdoor photography, start by setting your shutter speed to 1/125th of a second and the aperture to f-8. Preview the scene in your LCD monitor. If the image looks too dark, "open up" the aperture to f-5.6 or "slow down" the shutter speed to 1/60th of a second. You'll see the results of your adjustments in real time on the LCD monitor. If the scene is too bright, then "stop down" the aperture to f-11 or "speed up" the shutter to 1/250th of a second.

This is the beauty of manual mode photography; you have the option to adjust either the aperture or the shutter speed to reach the desired result. Sometimes aperture is more important, such as for portraits where you want to soften the background. In that case, set the aperture on f-2.8 (wide open) and change the shutter speed until the image looks correct in the LCD monitor.

Other times shutter speed might be more important, such as "stopping the action" during a sporting event: set the shutter speed at 1/500th of a second and adjust the aperture until the image looks properly exposed.

With a little practice, you'll find that manual exposure is an easy way for you to be in complete control of your digital camera.

Movie Mode

Digital still cameras are versatile imaging tools; many provide the option to capture short video clips, sometimes with sound. Typically, you access this function via the *Movie Mode* setting.

"Short" is the operative word here. Most cameras allow you to capture only 15 seconds of video at a time. After it captures the sequence, the camera then writes the data to the memory card and allows you to capture another 15 seconds until the memory card is full.

After you upload these video clips to your computer, you can stitch them together using a video editor such as QuickTime Pro. Standard size for these short movies is 320 pixels wide by 240 pixels tall. Typical frame rate is 15 frames per second (fps), which is half the speed of standard video, but still quite decent.

More advanced cameras enable you to capture longer sequences, sometimes up to three minutes, and usually with sound, via the microphone port located on the front of the camera. You can preview these mini-movies on your LCD monitor, and if you like them, you can post them to your personal web site or send them as email attachments.

For best image quality when shooting video, remember these tips:

Hold the camera steady during filming. Tripods are best for video shooting, but in a pinch, you can use your neck strap to stabilize the camera. Hold the camera out from your body until the strap is taut. Keep the camera in this position during filming, and it will help steady your shots.

Shoot in good lighting. Even more than with still photography, video requires good lighting. If your scene doesn't have enough ambient light, consider adding some with a video light.

Frame your subjects tight. Keep in mind that the final size of your movies is only 320 pixels wide and 240 pixels tall to begin with, so you can't afford to stand too far back from the action or your subjects will look the size of ants. Get close and shoot tight.

Your digital still camera probably won't replace a good video camcorder, but in a pinch it can capture a special moment that you would have otherwise missed.

Panorama Mode

If you want to capture the breadth of a scene, you most likely won't be able to fit all the grandeur into your camera's viewfinder—even at the wide angle setting. Have you ever remarked to someone viewing your vacation pictures, "It sure looked a lot more impressive when I was standing there"?

Panorama mode is a clever alternative offered by camera makers to help you capture the grandeur of big landscapes. The magic happens by photographing a sequence of images, then "stitching" them together later with your computer. Panorama mode prepares the sequence of shots for easy assemblage. Cameras that have this option also include the corresponding software required to make seamless final images, as seen in Figure 2-15.

Most panoramas require three to six images to achieve the full effect. When looking for good subjects, keep in mind that it's easier to create a seamless image when your subject is evenly illuminated. That usually means that the sun is to your back or off one shoulder. Avoid shooting directly into the sun for any of the frames in the sequence, at least until you're a little more experienced.

Then next trick is to keep the horizon line as level as possible as you capture each frame in the sequence. Tripods help tremendously with this task, but you might not always have one with you. So the next best solution is to become a *human tripod*. Here's how the technique works:

- Hold the camera firmly with both hands so you can see through the optical viewfinder or LCD monitor.

- Press your elbows against your body to create a steady support for the camera.

- Compose your first picture, usually starting from the left side. Note the location of the horizon line and make sure it's level.

- Take the first shot. After the shutter has fired, don't move!

- Continue to hold the camera in the locked elbow position and rotate your body a few degrees to the right to compose the next frame in the sequence. The only moving body parts should be your feet—everything else should be still as night. Make sure you have a 30 percent overlap from the previous image you shot—the computer uses this overlap information to stitch the pictures together.

- Check the horizon line to make sure it's in the same location as the last frame, and that it's still level.

Figure 2-15

This image of the Bay Bridge from San Francisco is actually six images "stitched" together using an Olympus C-3030 in panorama mode

- Take the second shot. (Don't move afterward!)
- Repeat this procedure through the entire sequence of shots.
- Turn off panorama mode once you've finished the series.

With a little practice, the human tripod technique will yield fantastic panoramas without lugging around your favorite three-legged friend.

One last thing to keep in mind is that panoramas are stunning as large prints. Shoot these sequences at your camera's highest resolution so you always have the option to print them at maximum size.

Programmed Exposure

The most common method for setting the aperture and shutter speed for digital cameras is *programmed auto exposure*. On many basic and intermediate models, this is the only exposure mode offered.

When using programmed exposure, all you have to do is "point and shoot." The camera's light meter "reads" the scene and compares that information to data stored in the camera's electronics. The camera then selects an aperture/shutter speed combination that best matches the information recorded by the light meter.

The caveat is that the camera's electronics can be fooled, resulting in a less-than-perfect picture. See the *Exposure Compensation* entry for more information on how to adjust programmed auto exposure to handle tricky lighting situations.

The bottom line is that programmed auto exposure is a reliable tool for capturing good pictures *most* of the time. You can increase your odds by learning a few of the override controls such as *exposure compensation*, *spot metering*, and *exposure lock*.

Protect Images

The Erase All command removes all images from your memory card. It's a handy way to clean house without having to remove each picture individually. What if, however, you wanted to remove all pictures except for one or two? The *Protect Images* option can help you do just that.

First, display the picture on the LCD monitor. Then choose "Protect Images" from the menu, and an icon should appear on the monitor, such as a key, to indicate that the picture is safe. Then you can use the Erase All command to delete the other images.

Be sure to practice this on test pictures to make sure everything works properly. Also, remember that Protect Images doesn't work when you use the Format Card command. All of your images will be erased, regardless of whether they are protected.

Resolution

By far one of the most important settings on your camera, *Resolution* sets the pixel dimensions of your picture, thereby determining how big it can be displayed or printed later on. See Figure 2-16.

If for example, you select your camera's smallest pixel dimensions—say, 640×480—your picture will be adequate for web page display. But if you wanted to make a photo-quality print of that picture, then you would only have enough resolution for a 3×4" print at best.

On the other hand, if you had selected your camera's maximum resolution, such as 1600×1200 pixels (on a 2 megapixel camera), then you could make a 5×7" photo quality print, or even a good 8 × 10" print from the same picture. (See table on page 14 for more detail.)

The tradeoff is that the higher the resolution, the more room each picture occupies on your memory card. So if you have a 2 megapixel camera with a 128MB memory card, you could squeeze 128 pictures on the card when the camera is set to its highest resolution (1600×1200 pixels). At medium resolution, 1024×768, your capacity increases to 271 pictures. And at the smallest resolution, 640×480, you can save a whopping 577 pictures to your card!

As tempting as 577 pictures sound, remember, if you take that once in a lifetime shot at 640×480, your once in a lifetime print will be wallet size. On the other hand, if you shoot at 1600×1200, you always have the option of making a nice 8×10" print, and if you just want to send images via email to friends and family, then scale down your "master" image to a smaller resolution before mailing.

For more information on preparing your pictures for email, see "Send Pictures Via Email" in Chapter 3.

Self Timer

The easiest way for you as the photographer to join a group shot is to use the camera's self timer, which delays the triggering the shutter (after you push the button) for 10 seconds or so.

Figure 2-16

Resolution menu: generally speaking, the higher settings are on the left, and
resolution declines as you move to settings on the right

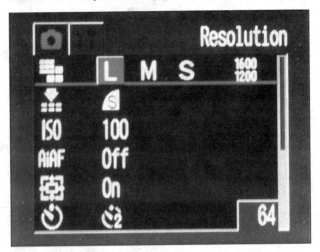

First, you position the camera on a solid surface or on a tripod, then
you compose the picture. Before firing away, activate the self timer. That
way, when you push the shutter button, the camera will count to 10
before taking the picture—giving you plenty of time to join your friends.

One of the tricks to self-timer mastery is to make sure the camera's
focusing sensor is reading the subjects and not the background. Be
especially careful when using the self timer for couples portraits,
because the sensor often reads the area right between their heads. If
your camera has *focus lock*, then you might want to use it. Using
manual focus is also handy for these types of shots, but only advanced
cameras offer this option.

The self timer can also be used as a substitute for a remote (or cable)
release, which comes in handy for pictures that require the shutter to
be open for a long time, such as a nighttime shot when the camera is
on a tripod. By using the self timer or remote release, you can trip the
shutter without vibrating the camera. Some cameras make this even
easier by providing you with a 2-second option to complement the

standard 10-second delay. That way you don't have to wait nearly as long for the shutter to trip once you've activated the timer.

Sequence Shooting

See *Burst/Continuous Shooting Mode* entry.

Shutter Priority

See *Timed Value (TV)* entry.

Spot Meter

This metering pattern enables you to "read" the exposure for a small area or "spot" in the viewfinder, usually in the center of the frame. Not all cameras include a spot meter option, but those that do enable the photographer to set the exposure on an element in the composition rather than the scene as a whole.

The most practical method for spot metering is to point the metering area at the object in the scene that is most important to you, then use exposure lock. Recompose the scene any way you want, knowing that the most important element in the picture will be exposed properly.

Timed Value (TV)

Sometimes referred to as *Shutter Priority*, this setting is often available on more advanced consumer models and all pro-level cameras. TV enables you to set the shutter speed and lets the camera figure out the corresponding aperture setting. A common use for TV is sports photography, in which the action is frozen with a "fast" shutter speed.

But TV is also useful for situations that demand a very slow shutter speed, such as to create a soft, dreamlike effect with running water. Here are a few scenarios where you might want to switch to shutter priority mode:

Sports event. A fast shutter speed of 1/500th or 1/1000th of a second will "stop the action." You'll need plenty of ambient light to use these settings. In a pinch, you can increase your *ISO Speed* setting to 400 to make your camera more light sensitive, but remember that you'll also lose some image quality by doing so.

Children playing outdoors. A fast shutter speed of 1/250th or 1/500th will help you record children at play. If you feel like you're missing good shots because of shutter lag (delay from the moment you press the shutter to when the picture is actually recorded), then try using *focus lock* to shorten lag time. You may also want to turn on the fill flash (see *Flash Modes*) and stay within 10 feet of your subjects. In addition to improving the lighting for outdoor portraits, flash helps freeze the action.

Running water. The effect you want determines the shutter speed you choose. If you want to freeze the water and see droplets suspended in air, use a fast shutter speed such as 1/250 or 1/500. If you shoot a waterfall and want a soft, dreamlike effect (see Figure 2-17), select a slow shutter speed such as 1/8. In this case, make sure you have your camera securely mounted on a tripod.

Figure 2-17

By using a slow shutter speed, the photographer was able to soften the appearance of the falling water. Exposure was set to 1 second. A polarizing filter was added to slow down the shutter and to help eliminate reflections

If the scene is too bright for you to use a slow shutter speed, then hold your sunglasses over the lens while making the exposure. Not only will this create a longer exposure, but you'll get a nice polarizing effect as a bonus! If your camera does accept accessory filters, then one of the best to have in your kit is a polarizer, which is much easier to use than holding sunglasses over the lens.

Streaking lights. To show motion, and this is particularly effective at twilight with car lights as they drive by, use a very slow shutter speed such as 2, 4, or even 8 seconds if your camera provides those options. Again, mounting your camera on a tripod is essential. If you have a remote release, then you might want to use it to prevent you from jarring the camera as you trip the shutter.

These examples don't cover every situation, but they will help you use shutter priority to create the effect you want when working with motion.

White Balance   WB

Different light sources, such as tungsten light bulbs, produce light at different color temperatures than normal daylight (different temperatures often result in pictures that are "cooler" or "bluish" in some situations, or "warmer" or "reddish" in others). Your optical/nervous system compensates for these variations in color, but cameras need a little help as you move from outdoors to in. Film cameras rely on color correction filters to capture natural tones under a variety of conditions. Digital cameras make things easier by providing a built-in *white balance* adjustment. This control not only allows you to capture pictures with accurate tones, but enables you to preview the effect on your LCD monitor before you take the shot.

The default setting for your camera is *auto white balance*. This mode works amazingly well most of the time. To test for yourself, point the camera at a different light source, such as a regular light bulb, and watch in the LCD monitor as the image slowly goes from very amber to a less surreal off-white.

The effect produced by auto white balance may not always be what you're looking for. In these instances, you can override the auto mode via one of the color correction presets available on your camera. Here's a list of the most common ones.

Daylight. Used for general outdoor photography. Adds a slight warmth to the coloring to offset a blue cloudless sky.

Cloudy. Helps correct overcast skies, but also good for shooting in open shade, such as under a tree. This setting adds more warmth to the scene than the daylight selection.

Tungsten. Offsets the reddish cast created by standard light bulbs by adding a bluish tone.

Fluorescent. Corrects for the greenish cast under warm-white or cool-white fluorescent tubes.

Fluorescent H. Helps balance the color for daylight fluorescent tubes.

Many intermediate to advanced cameras also include a custom white balance that allows the camera to find the right color correction when you point your camera at a white surface.

Even though these settings are designed to help you create as natural color as possible, you can also use them creatively. For example, if you were shooting a portrait indoors next to an open window, you would choose the cloudy setting to produce more natural skin tones. But what if you wanted to convey a more somber mood? By using the "tungsten" setting, the ambient light transforms to a bluish-colored hue, changing the mood of the entire shot.

The white balance settings are both practical and creative tools for the digital photographer.

Zoom/Magnify Control

Most people are familiar with using the zoom lever, or buttons, to zoom in and out when composing images in picture taking mode. But magnifying the picture you just captured on the LCD monitor for closer inspection is equally valuable.

The problem with LCD monitors is that they are very small, colorful, and sharp. What's wrong with that? If you don't "zoom in" when you review your pictures on these little screens, you might be misled as to the quality of your shots. In other words, LCD monitors make your pictures look better than they really are.

By using the magnify control to zoom in on your subject's face as you review the picture, you can get a better idea of its true quality. A perfect example is checking for correct exposure on the LCD monitor after you've taken a portrait. Much to your dismay, after you've uploaded the image to your computer, you see that the subject's eyes were closed. If you had used the magnify control right after you had taken the shot, you might have seen the closed eyes and continued the shoot.

Obviously, you don't want to employ the magnify control after every shot you take, but before you let your subject leave, take a few moments to review a sampling of the images so you know you won't be disappointed after you get home and upload the pictures.

Pulling It All Together

By now you've committed everything you learned in this section to memory, right? Probably not. That's why this book is a pocket guide and not a desktop reference. Keep it in your camera bag, backpack, or back pocket so you can refer to it over and over again.

As you continue to get comfortable with this information, you'll begin to use many of these functions in combination with one another to achieve the effect you want. For example, you may use both the *white balance* and *exposure compensation* adjustments to create a dark, moody indoor portrait. Then the next day, use the fill *flash mode* and *aperture priority* to shoot stunning bridal portraits at a wedding.

One of the advantages of digital photography is that you can experiment with these settings, and it doesn't cost you a penny. Plus, you get immediate feedback from your efforts.

The bottom line is to shoot, shoot, shoot. Have fun with the tools built into your camera, and learn to create images that express *your* vision and creativity.

CHAPTER 3

How Do I...
Tips and Tricks for Shooting and Sharing

By now you and your digital camera have become fast friends and are working together to make great images. But like the art of cooking, and life, there's always more to learn.

This chapter is more conversational than the previous two. The earlier sections of the book were designed for quick reference— to use while standing on the battlefield of photography and trying to survive. ("Quick, should I turn the flash on or off for my daughter's outdoor birthday party?" Answer: Flash on.)

But now the discussion becomes more free-flowing—like a conversation between two photographers trying to decide the best approach for a given situation. The topics in this chapter focus on both shooting and sharing pictures—what good is a great shot if you can't get it in front of others?

So, grab a fresh memory card, a charged set of batteries, and prepare for the next stage of your journey.

Shooting Tips and Tricks— How Do I...

How do I...? That's the question in photography, isn't it? Most of the time you know what you want to do: capture that sunset, take a pretty portrait, preserve the memory of that monument. The trick is to make the camera see it the way you do.

That's what you're going to learn here: the "how to" of photography. Not every situation is covered in this chapter, but if you master these techniques, there won't be too many pictures that get by your camera.

And when your friends mutter out loud something like, "How do I shoot that object inside the glass case?" You can reply, "Oh, that's easy. Just put the edge of the lens barrel against the glass to minimize reflections, then turn off the flash."

Take Great Outdoor Portraits

When most folks think of portrait photography, they envision studio lighting, canvas backdrops, and a camera perched upon a tripod. But many photographers don't have access to lavish professional studios, and honestly, it's not necessary for dynamite portraits.

PRO TIP

Figure 3-1 illustrates that you don't need an expensive photo studio to take pleasing outdoor portraits. After a little experimentation, a high camera angle was used to minimize distracting background elements. The model was positioned so the sun was on her back to create a rim lighting effect on the hair and shoulders. Then fill flash was added for even exposure on the face.

All you really need is a willing subject, a decent outdoor setting (preferably with trees), and your digital camera. Then you can be on your way to creating outstanding images.

First, start with the two magic rules for great outdoor portraits are:

Get close. The tighter you frame the shot, the more impact it will have. Extend your zoom lens and move your feet to create more powerful images. Once you've moved in close, and have shot a series of images, get closer and shoot again.

Use fill flash. Turning on the flash outdoors is a trick that wedding photographers have been using for years. If you really want to impress your subjects, position them in the

Figure 3-1

Outdoor portrait with fill flash and rim lighting (f-4 at 1/60th of a second)

open shade (such as under a tree) with a nice background in the distance. Then turn on the fill flash and make sure you're standing within 10 feet (so the flash can reach the subject). Your shots will be beautiful.

Once you've found a setting that you like and have everything in order, then "work the scene." Start by taking a few straight-forward images. Pay close attention while you have the model turn a little to the left, then to the right. When you see a position you like, shoot a few frames.

(Don't get too carried away with this "working the angles" thing, or people will hate you. You're not a swimsuit photographer on a *Sports Illustrated* location shoot. But the point is, don't be afraid to experiment with different camera positions. Just do it quickly.)

Then move in closer and work a few more angles. Raise the camera and have the model look upward; lower the camera and have the subject look away. Be sure to take lots of shots while experimenting with angles, because once you're finished shooting and review the images later on your computer screen, you'll discard many of the pictures that looked great on the camera's LCD monitor. The problem is that when they're enlarged, you'll see bothersome imperfections you didn't notice before.

PRO TIP

What if you need to take a portrait in a chaotic situation, such as this shot of an Olympic Torch carrier on a busy street (Figure 3-2)? One solution is to lower the camera angle and use the blue sky as the backdrop. Don't forget to turn on the fill flash!

Communicate with your subjects and try to put them at ease. Nobody likes the silent treatment from the photographer. It makes them feel like you're unhappy with how the shoot is going.

Here are a few other things to *avoid* when shooting outdoor portraits.

Avoid side lighting on women's faces. Light coming in from the side accentuates texture. That's the last thing most female models want to see in their shots because texture equates to skin aging or imperfections. Use a fill flash to minimize texture and avoid side lighting unless for special effect.

Figure 3-2

Low camera angle using the blue sky as a backdrop
(f-5.6 at 1/250th of a second; fill flash)

Don't show frustration. Never, ever, never make subjects feel
it's their fault that the shoot isn't going well. They're
already putting their self-confidence on the line by letting
you take their picture. Don't make them regret that

decision. When shots go well, credit goes to the models. When shots go bad, it's the photographer's fault. Keep your ego in check so theirs can stay intact.

Avoid skimping on time or the number of frames you shoot.
Your images may look good on that little 2" LCD monitor, but when you blow them up on the computer screen, you're going to see lots of things you don't like. Take many shots of each pose, and if you're lucky, you'll end up with a few you really like.

Don't torture models by making them look into the sun. Yes, you were told for years to shoot with the sun to your back. That rule was devised by the photographer, not the model. Blasting your subjects' retinas with direct sun is only going to make them squint and sweat (and swear). Be kind to your models and they'll reward you with great shots.

Avoid busy backgrounds. Bright colors, linear patterns, and chaotic landscape elements will detract from your compositions. Look for continuous tones without the hum of distracting elements.

Now that the basics are covered, here are a couple of super pro tips. These aren't techniques that you should use until you have good, solid shots recorded on your memory card. But once you do, maybe try these.

Soft background portraits. These are simply lovely. A soft, slightly out of focus background keeps the viewer's eye on the model and gives your shots a real professional look. The mechanics of this technique are described in Chapter 2 under "Aperture Priority Mode."

Rim lighting for portraits. When you place the sun behind the model, often you get highlights along the hair. Certain hairstyles really accentuate this effect. Remember to use fill flash for this setup or your model's face will be underexposed.

Set Up Group Shots

Many of the rules for engaging portraits apply to group shots too. So keep in mind everything that you've learned so far while preparing for this assignment.

PRO TIP

Figure 3-3 uses the classic "triangle" composition for a three-person group shot. Notice that distracting background elements are kept to a minimum. The subjects are positioned in the shade to eliminate harsh shadows on the face and squinty eyes. A fill flash is used for even front illumination.

Figure 3-3

Outdoor group shot beneath a shady tree with fill flash (f-5.6 at 1/80th of a second)

The first challenge is to arrange the group into a decent composition. If you've ever participated in a wedding, you know this drill.

Remind everyone in the shot that they need to have a clear view of the camera. If they can't see the camera, then the camera won't be able to see them. Next, position people as close as possible. Group shot participants tend to stand too far apart. That might look OK in real life, but the camera accentuates the distance between people and the result looks awkward. Plus, you can't afford to have this shot span as wide as a football field, or you'll never see people's faces unless you enlarge the image to poster size.

Remember to take lots of shots—for large groups, a minimum of five frames. This gives you a chance to overcome blinking eyes, sudden head turns, bad smiles, and unexpected gusts of wind ruining your pictures.

Before pressing the shutter button, quickly scan the group looking for little annoyances that will drive you crazy later: crooked ties, sloppy hair, and turned-up collars will make you insane during post production.

Finally, work quickly. You're not John Ford making the great American epic, so don't act like it. Keep things moving for the sake of your subjects (and for your own tired feet).

Capture Existing-Light Portraits

By now you've probably realized one of the great ironies in good portrait photography: you should turn the flash on when working outdoors. So guess what the great secret is for indoor portraiture? That's right; turn the flash off. Some of the most artistic portraits use nothing more than an open window and a simple reflector.

The problem with using your on-camera flash indoors is that the light is harsh and creates a very contrasty image. "Harsh" and "contrasty" are not two words models like to hear when describing the pictures you've just taken of them.

Fill flash works outdoors because everything is bright. The flash "fills" right in. But ambient light is much dimmer indoors, and the burst of light from the flash is much like a car approaching on a dark street.

PRO TIP

Using on-camera flash indoors for portraits (Figure 3-4) creates harsh highlights and ugly shadows on the backdrop. It's nice to have the built-in flash in a pinch, but you don't want to make a habit of using it for indoor portraits.

Of course there are times when you have no choice but to use your camera's flash indoors. It's very convenient, and you do get a recognizable picture. But when you have the luxury of setting up an artistic portrait in a window-lit room, try existing light only.

PRO TIP

Using the light from an open window creates a more flattering portrait (Figure 3-5). The camera is on a tripod for steadiness during the long exposure, and reflectors are positioned on both sides of the model to minimize deep shadows.

First, position the model near an open window and study the scene. You can't depend solely on your visual perception, because your eyes and brain are going to read the lighting a little differently than the camera will, especially in the shadow areas—you will see detail in the dark areas that the camera can't record.

This is why you need a reflector to "bounce" some light into the shadow areas. Many photographers swear by collapsible light discs, but a large piece of white cardboard or foam core will work just as well.

Place your reflector opposite the window and use it to "bounce" the light on to the dark side of the model. This will help "fill in" the shadow area so you can see some detail.

Figure 3-4

On-camera flash produces harsh results for indoor portraits and should be avoided as much as possible (f-2.5 @ 1/60th of a second)

Figure 3-5

Existing light portrait shot in the same setting as Figure 3-4, but with the flash turned off (f-2.5 @ 1/4th of a second, ISO speed set at 50)

Figure 3-6 shows the existing light setup for Figure 3-5. The model is facing the window with reflectors positioned on both sides of her. The blank wall serves as the backdrop, and the camera is secured on a tripod.

Figure 3-6

The existing light setup used for Figure 3-5 (f-2.5 @ 1/4th of a second, ISO speed set at 50)

Now put your camera on a tripod and slowly squeeze the shutter button. Review the image on the LCD monitor. If the shadow area is too dark, you may want to add another reflector. If the overall image is too dark, turn on exposure compensation, set it to +1, and try another picture. If the color balance of the image is too "cool" (that is, bluish), then you may want to set the White Balance control to "cloudy" and see if that improves the rendering.

Remind your model to sit very still during exposure because you may be using a shutter speed that's as slow as 1/15th of a second, or even longer.

You could increase the camera's light-sensitivity by adjusting the ISO speed to 200, but don't go beyond that because you'll degrade the image quality too much for this type of shot.

Once you've played with these variables, go back to the artistic side of your brain and work on the composition. Try to get all the elements in the picture working together and let nature's sweet light take it from there. When it all comes together, existing light portraits are magical.

Shoot Good Self-Portraits

Some people may think that turning the camera toward yourself is the height of narcissism, but sometimes you need a shot, and no one is around to take it for you. These are the times when it's good to know how to shoot a self-portrait.

Start with the basics by making sure your hair is combed, collar is down, shirt is clean, and your teeth are free from spinach (and lipstick!). Then find a location with a pleasing, uncluttered background. Put the camera on a tripod and set the focus as close to the area where you'll be standing or sitting and activate the self timer. If the room is too dim for an existing light portrait, try using "slow-synchro" flash (see "Flash Modes" in Chapter 2 for more information). This type of flash provides enough illumination for a good portrait, but slows the shutter enough to record the ambient light in the room. Position yourself where you had focused the camera and look directly into the lens. Don't forget to smile.

When setting up a self-portrait, pay attention to background elements so they don't distract too much from the main subject: you! If you have to use flash, try slow-synchro mode to preserve the room ambience (see Figure 3-7).

Figure 3-7

Self-portrait indoors using the flash set in slow-synchro mode (f-2.5 @ 1/30th of a second)

Take several shots, trying different poses until you hit on a few you like. If you have a remote release for your camera, you can save yourself lots of running back and forth from the tripod to the modeling position.

Creative portraits are sometimes more fun when you're both photographer and model. In Figure 3-8, the rearview mirror of a car is used to frame this self-portrait.

Figure 3-8

**Self-portrait using the rear view mirror of a car
(f-2.8 @ 1/20th of a second, no flash)**

Self-portraits are also perfect for experimenting with different "looks" that might make you feel more self conscious when someone else is behind the camera. You can try different expressions and poses, and erase the bad ones. The world will never know the difference.

Take Interesting Kid Shots

Children are a challenge for digital cameras, primarily because of shutter lag. In short, kids move faster than digicams can react. But with a few adjustments, you can capture excellent images that you'll cherish for years.

One of the most important adjustments, regardless of the type of camera you're using, is to get down to kid level when shooting. This is "hands and knees" photography at its best. And if you need to, get on your belly for just the right angle. By doing so, your shots will instantly become more engaging.

Next, get close. Then get closer. This may seem impossible at times with subjects who move so fast, but if you want great shots, then you've got to keep your subjects within range.

PRO TIP

Kids are a challenge for digital cameras, but if you use focus lock, fill flash, and work at their level, you can capture pleasing shots (Figure 3-9) throughout their years.

Figure 3-9

**Go where the kids are to get good shots
(f-4 @ 1/250th of a second, fill flash and focus lock)**

Now turn on the flash, regardless of whether you're indoors or out. Not only will this provide even illumination, but flash helps "freeze" action, and you'll need all the help you can get in this category.

Finally, use the "focus lock" technique described in the practical example "Capturing the Decisive Moment" in Chapter 2. By doing so, you can reduce shutter lag and increase your percentage of good shots.

Some of the most rewarding pictures you'll ever record will be of children. Like the child-rearing process itself, kid photography requires patience. But the results far surpass the effort.

Capture Engaging Travel Portraits

Make sure you pack a spare memory card and extra batteries when you hit the road with your digital camera, because these compact picture-takers are perfect travel companions.

The best portraits on the road usually consist of two shots. The first frame, often called the *establishing shot*, is of the point of interest itself, such as an old church. Then the second image is a nicely framed portrait with an *element of the structure* included in the picture.

Why two shots? For the same reason that movie makers use this technique. If you were to include the entire structure and the model in the establishing shot, the model would be unrecognizable. That's the problem with so many vacation shots—they're taken at too great a distance.

PRO TIP

You can't capture the grandeur of great buildings and monuments, and take a portrait, in the same shot. Can you find the model in Figure 3-10? Look in the oval.

On the other hand, if you shoot all of your travel portraits tightly framed only, your viewers won't know the difference between Denmark and Detroit. By using the two-shot method you establish the scene and capture an engaging portrait. Figure 3-11 illustrates the two-shot method.

One last note: don't forget to take pictures of signs and placards. It's a lot easier than taking notes, and the information comes in very handy when recounting your travel experiences.

Figure 3-10

The model is dwarfed within this travel shot of a beautiful mission (f-4.7 @ 1/600th of a second)

Figure 3-11

Once you've captured the establishing shot, you can move in close for the portrait–even if it's of an architectural element

Take Pictures at Weddings

Weddings are portrait heaven. Your subjects look sharp, are happy, and are in pretty settings. All you have to do is have your camera ready for the opportunities as they present themselves.

Rule one is to not interfere with the hired photographer's shots. If you want to "follow in his wake" for special posed portraits, simply ask permission to shoot a couple frames after he finishes. Most pros will accommodate these polite requests.

Next, turn on your flash and leave it on—indoors or out. See "Flash Modes" in Chapter 2 for an overview of your options and how to use them.

When you're taking group shots, remember to position guests as closely as possible. Generally speaking, people stand too far apart. Get them close together.

Make sure everyone in the group has a clear view of the camera. If they can't see the camera, then the camera can't see them. If you have to, stand on a stable chair to get a better angle for group shots. The choice for large groups is simple: either you vary the heights of those in the group by using steps or risers, or you raise the camera angle above their heads and shoot downward.

Keep an eye out for candids too. Look for those special moments that make these gatherings so memorable—a kiss on the cheek, a sleepy child in a guest's arms, the perfect toast, a romantic dance sequence, and guests signing in are potential great photographs just waiting for you to shoot.

PRO TIP

When taking pictures at weddings, don't forget to keep your eyes open for candids, like Figure 3-12. They are often the most interesting shots of the day.

Figure 3-12

**Wedding candids are often the most interesting shots of the day
(f-2 @ 1/60th of a second)**

Finally, don't forget to include props in the shots when available. A hint of wedding cake in the background or a beautiful flower arrangement could be the frosting to add the perfect finish to your portrait.

Prevent Red Eye

Your subjects are vulnerable to red eye in dimly lit rooms when their pupils are open wide. The effect is actually caused by the light from the flash bouncing off the retina and reflecting back into the picture taking lens. Point-and-shoot cameras are notorious for causing red eye, because the flash is so close to the lens, making a perfect alignment to catch the reflection from the retina.

Even though many cameras provide a setting to reduce red eye (see "Flash Modes" in Chapter 2), they don't always work well, and actually can be irritating to both subject and photographer. A better way is to incorporate as many of these tips as possible when shooting in low light.

- Have the model look directly at a light source, such as a lamp, before taking the shot. This will constrict the pupils and reduce red eye.
- Turn up the room lights if possible.
- Shoot off to the side of the subject, or have the model look a little to the left or the right of the camera, but not directly at the lens.
- Use an external flash mounted on a bracket. This is how wedding photographers cope with this problem. It works by changing the angle of reflection from the retina.
- Try an existing light portrait, if the conditions are suitable.

If all else fails, you can touch up the photograph in an image editor after uploading. It's not a perfect solution, but easier than it used to be, thanks to more friendly computer technology (for help with touching up red eye, try *iPhoto: The Missing*

Manual or *Photoshop Elements 2: The Missing Manual*, both from Pogue Press).

Take Pictures from the Stands of Sporting Events

Speaking of flash, how many times have you seen hundreds of cameras firing off from the stands during a sporting event in a large stadium? Alas, what a waste of film.

The flash distance for most point-and-shoot cameras is about 10 feet. That means if you're shooting from the stands, you're illuminating a couple rows of seats in front of you, and that's about it.

Instead, *turn off your flash* and use existing light techniques. If you can adjust your camera's ISO setting (see "ISO Speed" in Chapter 2), then bump it up to 200 or 400. This will increase your camera's light sensitivity.

PRO TIP

When you're sitting in the cheap seats, forget about using your flash. Existing light photography is your best bet (Figure 3-13) for bringing home a souvenir.

When you take the shot, hold the camera very steady, because the shutter speed will be slow, and you'll want to minimize *camera shake*, which degrades image quality. Better yet, use a tripod if the situation allows.

Even if you hold the camera steady, the action on the playing field will blur, so try to make your exposures right after, or before, the action.

Obviously, you're not going to get *Sports Illustrated* shots from the cheap seats. But for memorable occasions, such as Barry Bonds hitting his 600th home run, it's great to have a few well-exposed images from the event to keep in the scrapbook.

Figure 3-13

Turn off the flash and find a good vantage point when shooting from the stands (1/40th of a second at f-3.5 with the flash turned off using a Canon PowerShot S200)

Capture Action Shots

The three keys to capturing effective action shots are to shoot at your camera's highest resolution, use a fast shutter speed, and take measures to reduce shutter lag.

First, set your camera at its highest resolution. You will probably want to "crop in" your image later to bring the action closer. Having extra pixels actually extends the reach of your lens, which is very helpful for this type of photography. See Figures 3-14 and 3-15 for examples of moving closer by cropping.

The key to "stopping action," such as capturing a bird in flight, is to use a fast shutter speed setting. Typically, you should use a speed of at least 1/250th, 1/500th, or 1/1000th of a second. The programmed auto exposure mode on most digital cameras is calibrated to give you the fastest shutter speed possible, so you don't need to monkey too much with your camera settings when going after action shots.

But what you really need is lots of light. The brightest hours of the day are best, usually from 9:00 a.m to 4:00 p.m. Shooting outdoors during this times should produce shutter speeds of 1/250th of a second or faster. If you have Shutter Priority mode, you can set the speed yourself and let the camera handle the corresponding aperture setting.

PRO TIP

Here's an example of how to capture action shots with your digital camera. The shot in Figure 3-14 of an egret in flight was captured with an Olympus C3030Z with an 1.4x telephoto attachment over the lens. "Panning" was used to follow the bird as it flew overhead. The focus was locked on infinity to eliminate auto focus activity. The shutter speed was a fast 1/500th of a second to "freeze" the action. Because the original image was shot at a full 3 megapixels, there was enough resolution to crop out much of the sky, creating a more dynamic shot.

Unfortunately, a fast shutter speed doesn't help you overcome the lag time that exists between the moment you press the picture-taking button and when the shutter actually fires. *Shutter lag* is the nemesis of action photographers, and it's the number one complaint about digital cameras from consumers too.

Most digicams have two features that can help you combat shutter lag. The first is *burst mode*, which allows you to take a rapid sequence of shots. If you start the sequence right as the action is initiated, then your odds of capturing the decisive moment is much higher. (See "Burst/Continuous Shooting Mode" in Chapter 2.)

Figure 3-14

Uncropped photo of egret flying overhead. Megapixels do matter. If this
original shot of the egret in flight hadn't been captured at a full 3 megapixels,
then there wouldn't have been enough image information to allow for
cropping, as illustrated in Figure 3-15.

The other trick is to "preset the focus," thereby disabling the
auto focus system and shortening the lag time between pressing the picture-taking button and actually recording the
picture. The best way to do this is to use a function called *infinity lock*. The camera "locks in" the focus at infinity, which provides you a range from about 10 feet to forever. Once infinity
lock is engaged, you can fire at will without relying on the auto
focus system. Sometimes you have to switch to Landscape
mode in order to activate the infinity lock. This step doesn't
seem intuitive, but often it works. For more information on
this function, see the "Infinity Lock" section in Chapter 2.

Figure 3-15

Action shot of egret in flight (Olympus C3030Z, 1.4X telephoto attachment, f-5 @ 1/500th of a second)

Another helpful technique for action shooting is called *panning*, in which you "follow" the moving subject during exposure. Using this technique may feel odd at first, because you're taught to always hold the camera as still as possible when taking the picture. But panning can provide stunning results; if you follow the subject accurately, it will be in focus while the background displays motion blur. This effect gives the photograph great energy and a sense of movement.

The classic panning exercise is to have a bicyclist ride by while you keep the camera fixed on the rider during exposure. Use focus lock and burst mode to give yourself the best odds for timing the shot correctly. You might not be able to fully appreciate the effect on your small LCD monitor, but when you upload the images to you computer you'll see this wonderfully blurred background providing the sensation of motion. Give it a try!

Shoot in Museums

Museums, aquariums, and natural habitat parks provide opportunities for unusual shots. They also present some difficult challenges for the digital photographer, but nothing that can't be overcome with a little ingenuity.

Before you get too excited at the prospects of shooting beautiful works of art in a museum, be sure to ask if it's OK. Often you'll discover that photography is allowed in some areas and not in others. To avoid embarrassing confrontations, ask when you first enter the facility.

Even when you're granted permission, you'll probably be told that you can't use a flash, and you're not allowed to set up a tripod. Here are a few tips to help you work around those constraints.

First, check your *white balance*. Chances are your images are displaying a noticeable reddish hue in your LCD monitor. Try using the Tungsten setting to improve the color balance. Some cameras allow you to set a custom color balance setting. You might want to give that a try if the presets don't provide the results you want. For more information, see "White Balance" in Chapter 2.

Next, you're going to have to find a way to combat the low ambient light often found inside museums. Chances are the *camera shake* symbol is flashing on your LCD monitor telling you that your pictures are going to be "soft" due to a slow shutter speed.

If your camera has a neck strap, you can use it to help you steady the shots. Pull the camera out from your body until the strap is taut. Use this resistance to steady your hands as you make the exposure. If available, you can also lean against a wall or a pillar to help you combat camera shake.

As a last resort, you can increase your camera's light sensitivity by adjusting the ISO setting. Changing the setting to 200 or

400 might get rid of the camera shake warning, but your picture quality won't be as good. For more information, see "ISO Speed" in Chapter 2.

Regardless of the type of museum you're visiting, you're probably going to encounter glass cases and exhibits behind glass. The trick to eliminating unwanted reflections is to put the outer edge of camera lens barrel right up against the glass, hold the camera steady, then shoot. By putting the lens barrel close to the glass, you eliminate those nasty room reflections that often ruin otherwise beautiful shots.

PRO TIP

Shooting through exhibit glass can mean unwanted reflections appear in your pictures. This image (Figure 3-16) of a moon jelly was shot through aquarium glass, but the edge of the camera's lens barrel was gently placed directly on the glass of the exhibit, thereby eliminating unwanted reflections. Because the ambient light was low, the ISO setting had to be increased to 400 in increase the camera's sensitivity. Remember, you have to turn off your flash to use this technique.

Once you upload your pictures from your visit to the museum, you'll probably notice that many of images will suffer from softness and other maladies that you didn't detect in the LCD monitor. Don't despair, though—even if only a fraction of your images survive, they'll be treasured for years to come, and are well worth the effort of capturing.

Shoot Architecture Like a Pro

Adding pictures of buildings and their interesting elements to your travel pictures brings another dimension to your presentations. Point-and-shoot cameras aren't ideal for architectural shooting, but by following these suggestions, you'll be surprised by the results you can achieve.

Figure 3-16

Moon jelly through glass aquarium (f-2.2 @ 1/50th of a second, ISO 400, no flash, white balance set to cloudy)

You may have noticed a phenomenon called *converging lines* when taking pictures of large buildings. Instead of the structure standing straight and tall, it looks distorted. This effect is caused when the plane of the camera isn't parallel to the plane of the building. The problem of nonparallel planes is caused by shooting upward at a tall structure (the building is standing at a 90 degree angle, and your camera is most likely angled 45 degrees or so). By angling your camera upward to frame the shot, you create distortion because the planes of the camera and the building are not parallel.

One trick is to elevate your height so you can point the camera straight at the building instead of upward (both camera and building are angled at 90 degrees). Maybe you can go over to a building across the way and shoot through an open window from the second or third floor. Look for positions that allow you to shoot "across" instead of "upward" if you want to eliminate distortion.

In Figure 3-17, the tall buildings are standing straight because the shot was taken from the seventh floor of a hotel
across the way. The camera was positioned on a tripod so it
was perfectly parallel to structures in the composition.

Figure 3-17

Tall buildings are standing straight because the plane of the camera is parallel
to the plane of the structures (f-2 @ 1 second, no flash, ISO 50)

But don't limit yourself to shooting only the big picture: architectural elements are often just as interesting if not more so
than the complete structure. And the best part is that distortion is much easier to control with smaller elements than with
the entire building.

Look for interesting designs around windows, over doors, and
along the roof line. Zoom in on specific areas that interest
you—elements that you might have missed during casual
observation.

PRO TIP

Sometimes the parts make more interesting pictures than the whole. In Figure 3-18, early morning sidelight emphasizes the texture and depth of this church.

To enhance textures and depth, look for "side lighting" that often provides more interesting images than flat front lighting. And don't forget to grab a couple snaps of signs and placards to help you tell the story once you return home.

(Remember, *side lighting* is good for buildings because it enhances texture, but not so good for people, for the same reason.)

Shoot Items Using Tabletop Photography

There are two ways to shoot items using tabletop photography: the hard way and the easy way. The hard way involves multiple studio lights, soft boxes, umbrellas, and seamless backdrop paper. Professionals use this equipment to produce outstanding images for commercial advertising and high-end editorial work.

But if you just want a nice picture of your old 35mm camera to sell on eBay, you probably don't want to set up an entire studio. So here's the easy way.

First, find a window you can set a table next to. North-facing windows are great but not necessary for this type of shooting. Cover the surface with white paper, and if you can, create a white backdrop too. This will be your work area.

Now put your camera on a tripod and adjust it so it's facing the item that you want to photograph on the table. Move both the subject and the camera to achieve the best lighting possible via the open window. Once everything is in place, make a tabletop reflector out of white cardboard or cover a card with aluminum foil. Position the reflector opposite the light source (window) so it's bouncing light on to the shadow side of the item.

Figure 3-18

Church shot in morning side lighting (f-4.5 @ 1/640th of a second)

PRO TIP

Your photo studio for tabletop photography can consist of nothing more than a table next to a window, a tripod, and a couple of reflectors (see result in Figure 3-19).

Figure 3-19

Natural light studio shot (f-3.5 @ 1/100th of a second, no flash)

Adjust your white balance to Cloudy (see "White Balance" in Chapter 2 for more information) and put your camera on self timer (see "Self Timer" in Chapter 2). Now, trip the timer and stand back. After 10 seconds or so, the camera will take the shot for you to review. Continue refining your setup until you get the shot you want.

This simple setup can produce studio-like results at a fraction of the cost or effort. Give it a try.

Create Powerful Landscape Images

You could spend your entire lifetime studying how to make great landscape images. There are, however, a few key techniques that will improve your nature shots right away while you learn the subtleties of the craft. Here are a few tips to keep in the back of your mind while shooting.

Work with magic light. Landscape pictures shot *before 9:00 a.m.* and *after 5:00 p.m.* look better, especially with digital cameras that have a hard time taming harsh midday sun.

Keep your compositions simple. Clutter is the bane of powerful landscape imagery. Look for simple, powerful compositions, and skip the rest.

Use a tripod when possible. By keeping your camera rock steady, you will squeeze every bit of sharpness out of the lens, rendering even the tiniest elements with clarity. Plus, photographers who use tripods tend to study their scenes more and have more refined compositions.

Be patient. Sometimes you have to wait for nature to paint you the perfect picture. Allow enough time to stay put for a while and watch the light change.

Use a polarizing filter. If your camera accepts accessories such as auxiliary lenses and filters, then consider adding a polarizing filter to your bag of tricks. Polarizers remove unwanted reflections, deepen color saturation, and bring an overall clarity to the scene. The effect is strongest when the sunlight is coming into the scene from over your shoulder.

Protect against lens flare by shielding the front glass element of your camera from the sun. Lens flare is that demon that degrades the color saturation of your images. Lens hoods were once standard issue for 35 mm cameras, but now no one seems to use them for digitals. To improve the quality of your shots, make sure the sun is not reflecting off the front of your lens. If it is, then shield it with your hand, or better yet, this book, which is a perfect size for the job.

Shoot at the highest resolution and sharpness your camera allows. Landscapes look best when printed big. But to do so, you need all the resolution your camera can muster.

Get out and walk. If you see a good shot from the seat of your car, chances are it's even better a few hundred yards away from the road.

Don't increase your ISO speed setting to cope with low light.
Bumping your speed will degrade the quality of your image. Use a tripod and your self timer instead.

PRO TIP

The lake and mountain landscape shown in Figure 3-20 was taken after 5:00 p.m. with a handheld digital camera.

Figure 3-20

Lake and mountain landscape (f-7 @ 1/500th of a second)

By keeping these tips in mind, and by reviewing the "Composition" section in Chapter 2, you can begin learning the craft of landscape photography with your digital point-and-shoot camera, and take some great shots while doing so.

Take Flash Pictures of People Who Blink at Flash

Every now and then you'll run into someone whose eyes are very sensitive to flash and who has a knack for blinking right as the flash fires. The result is a series of unflattering facial expressions and lots of frustration.

One of the best tricks to help calm the nerves of model and photographer alike is to use the red eye reduction mode. (See "Flash Modes" in Chapter 2 and "Prevent Red Eye" earlier in this chapter for more information). The pre-flash that is designed to reduce red eye will actually cause the model to blink early; then, their eyes will be open when the exposure takes place. It works almost every time.

Computer Tips and Tricks: How Do I …

You've just returned from a great two-week vacation with memory cards bursting at the seams. Now what do you do?

Before you spam every friend and relative you know with triple-megapixel masters, take a few minutes to learn about *sampling down* images so they have smaller file sizes, and archiving pictures so you can find them months later when you want to relive the great memories.

In other words, this section will help you keep your friends happy and your pictures safe and sound.

Send Pictures Via Email

One of the first things that new digital camera owners love to do is send a batch of images to family members or friends. As you may have already discovered yourself, the warmth of the reception is inversely proportional to the size of the images that land in their inbox.

All too many times budding photographers send full-sized 1-, 2-, or even 3-megapixel pictures as email attachments that take forever to download and are too large to view comfortably on the computer monitor.

Indeed, you should shoot at your camera's highest resolution, but remember not to send those full-sized images to others. All parties concerned will be much happier if you create a much smaller "email version" of your pictures and send those along.

Use your image editor to resize *a copy* for easier handling. To do so, use the Save As command in your image editor. The largest size you should send as an email attachment is 640×480 pixels, and 320×240 pixels will usually do the job.

If you're lucky enough to have Photoshop (or Photoshop Elements) as your image editor, then use the Image Size function to resize the picture. (Other image editors have similar functions, too!) When you first open the Image Size dialog box, you'll see the current width and height of the picture. In the settings in Figure 3-21, the dimensions are 2,272 pixels wide by 1,704 pixels tall. This shot was taken at full resolution with a 4-megapixel camera. If you sent this picture as is, the file size would be well over 1 megabyte even after compression, and a full 11 megabytes when opened. That's not the kind of attachment you want to send to friends and family.

But after using image size to reduce the pixel dimensions to 320×240, the compressed file size shrank to under 100 kb—that's less than 1/10th the size of the original image!

Make sure you have both the Constrain Proportions and Resample Image boxes checked when preparing image copies for email. With the Constrain Proportions box checked, Photoshop automatically changes the height dimension for you.

Figure 3-21

The Image Size dialog box in Photoshop 7

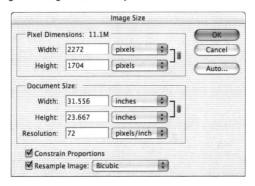

PRO TIP

"Resampling" may be one of those words you've heard before, but you're not quite sure what it means. In simplest terms, resampling means that the image editor is either *adding* or *subtracting* pixels to the image. Usually you want to avoid "sampling up," that is, adding pixels, because that degrades image quality. But "sampling down" or subtracting pixels, is a great way to reduce the file size of image copies that you want to send via email or post on the Web. In other words, when you change the *Width* and *Height* dimensions to smaller numbers, such as 320×240, you're *sampling down*, and both the picture and the file size will be smaller (Figure 3-22).

If you have a choice, the best image format to use for email attachments is JPEG (*.jpg*). When saving in this format, you will usually be asked (by your computer) which level of compression you want to use. Generally speaking, *medium* or *high* gives you the quality you need.

Remember to keep your original image safe and sound so you can use it later for printing and large display. To help eliminate confusion when dealing with these different sizes, you might want to save two copies, calling one *vacation one hires.jpg* and the more compact version *vacation one lores.jpg*.

Figure 3-22

Appropriate dimensions for emailing pictures entered into the Image Size dialogue box in Photoshop 7

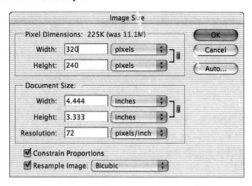

By sending friends and family smaller, more manageable pictures, you'll hear more about how beautiful your shots are, and less about how long the darn thing took to download.

Get Photo-Quality Prints

There are a variety of ways to get photo-quality prints from your digital images. You can do them yourself with an inkjet printer, or have a photo finisher do the work for you.

Many camera stores offer photo finishing from digital images. Simply take in your memory card, order your prints, and pick them up the next day.

You can also order prints through online services such as Shutterfly (*http://www.shutterfly.com*). You have to upload your pictures via the Internet to their facility, then they send the prints back through the mail.

Either camera-store or online service make the most sense for photographers with busy schedules. On occasion, you may want to run a few pictures through the inkjet printer at home, but generally speaking, professional services are more convenient, and the prints are of higher quality.

Present a Digital Slideshow

Presenting slideshows on a given subject is an age-old photographic tradition. Digital cameras make it easier than ever to present your images to many people at once.

Many digicams have "video out" capability that enable you to connect your camera directly to a television for playback on a large screen. If your camera has this functionality, then it most likely has a slideshow mode that allows you to choose images that are stored on the memory card and present them on the television in timed intervals. All you have to do is turn on the stereo for some background music add a little witty commentary, and you have a full-fledged multimedia presentation to share with others.

Another option is to use the software that comes with your camera to assemble slideshows on the computer, then show them either on the computer monitor or connect the computer to a television for big screen presentations.

Computer slideshows have the advantage of being able to add transitions and special effects to the presentation. They can also be saved and played long after the memory card has been erased and reused.

You can also use independent software that didn't come with your camera for this purpose. Apple Computer's iPhoto not only enables you to make slide shows from your digital images, but also allows you to incorporate music directly into the presentation. You can even save the show as a QuickTime movie and send it to others.

Regardless of which method you use to create your presentations, keep these basic tips in mind to make your shows engaging, and leave your audience begging for more.

· Include only your best images.
· Tell a story with your pictures as well as with your words.

- Keep your presentations short. Ten to twenty minutes is all the time that's usually needed, or wanted, by your audience.

- Add music and anecdotes for more interest.

- Be creative. Add close-ups, distance shots, low angles, and high angles for variety.

- Never apologize for your pictures. If you don't think it's good enough to be in your show, then don't include it.

Slideshows have never been easier to create, and people do like them when they're done well.

Archive for Future Use

Digital images should be treated like any other important computer file: archived and kept in a safe place. Most computers these days have built-in CD-RW drives for burning compact discs, and CDs are an excellent archiving medium.

When preparing to back up your important photographs, take a few minutes to figure out how you want to organize your files before you start burning CDs. Since digital cameras usually assign names such as *IMG_3298.JPG* to your pictures, you won't be able to go back and find those Paris shots by reading the filenames. But you're probably not going to want to rename each picture individually either.

Instead, give a descriptive name to the folder that contains images of a like kind, such as *Paris Trip 2002*. You can always browse the contents of the folder with an image browser once you're in the general vicinity.

Regardless of which method you embrace, the important thing is that you have some system, and back up your files on a regular basis. You already know how frustrating it is to look for an old picture buried in a shoebox deep within your closet. Consider digital photography your second chance in life, and take advantage of your computer's ability to store and retrieve information.

Where to Go From Here

Now it's time to shoot. The best thing about digital cameras is that you can take picture after picture without worrying about film processing costs. And the best way to learn the art and science of photography is to take lots of pictures.

Keep your eyes open, your camera steady, and most importantly: enjoy.

Quick Reference Charts

The following tables can serve as a quick reference guide for a variety of camera settings. For more detailed explanations for the data listed here, see Chapter 2.

Table A-1. Exposure compensation reference guide

Lighting situation	Recommended exposure compensation (via the scale setting)
Subject against a bright sky background (high clouds on sunny day).	Overexpose by 2 (+2.0); use fill flash if within 10 feet
Light object (white color), front lit.	Overexpose by 1.5 (+1.5)
Subject against white sand or snow (e.g., person skiing).	Overexpose by 1.5 (+1.5)
Landscape scene dominated by bright, hazy sky.	Overexpose by 1 (+1.0)
Fair-skinned subjects with bright front lighting.	Overexpose by .5 (+.5)
Subject against green foliage in open sun (e.g., outdoor portrait with background trees and shrubs).	No compensation
Dark-skinned subjects with bright front lighting.	Underexpose by .5 (−.5)
Brightly lit subject against dark background (e.g., theater lighting).	Underexpose by 1 (−1.0)
Dark object (black color) front lit.	Underexpose by 1.5 (−1.5)

Table A-2. Flash mode settings

Situation	Recommended flash mode
Outdoor portrait in open shade or sun.	Fill flash (flash forced on)[a]
Subject against bright background such as hazy sky.	Fill flash (flash forced on)[a]
Wedding and other special events (both indoor and outdoor shooting).	Fill flash (flash forced on)
Subject in brightly lit evening scene such as Times Square, NYC, or Sunset Strip, LV.	Slow synchro flash
Portrait against twilight sky, brightly lit monument, or building.	Slow synchro flash
Portrait in brightly lit room where ambient lighting needs to be preserved.	Slow synchro flash[a]
Subject who typically blinks as flash fires.	Red eye reduction flash (to eliminate recorded blinking)
Mood portrait by window, bright lamp, or other similar setting.	Flash off (steady camera with tripod or other support)
Sporting event or outdoor concert when shooting from the stands.	Flash off (steady camera with tripod or other support)

[a] On some point-and-shoot cameras, these flash settings are only accessible when you enable Manual Mode. Cameras typically ship in Automatic Mode, which limits the number of adjustments that the photographer can change. Refer to your owners manual for more information.

Table A-3. White balance settings

Lighting condition	Recommended White Balance setting
Sunny, outdoor conditions.	Auto or Daylight
Open shade (e.g., under a tree), indoor portraits by window light, or when flash is on indoors.	Cloudy (add fill flash when possible)
Snow setting, bluish winter light, or when overall light balance is too "cool."	Cloudy
Indoors with flash off and tungsten light is the dominate light source.	Tungsten

Table A-3. White balance settings (continued)

Lighting condition	Recommended White Balance setting
Outdoors at sunset or sunrise when light is too "warm."	Tungsten
Indoors when dominant light source is fluorescent tubes.	Fluorescent

Table A-4. Camera modes with explanation

Camera mode[a]	Explanation
Programmed Auto (P)	Camera sets both aperture and shutter speed. Good for general photography.
Shutter Priority/ Timed Value (TV)	Photographer sets the shutter speed and the camera sets corresponding aperture. Best for action, sports, running water photography.
Aperture Priority/ Aperture Value (AV)	Photographer sets the aperture (f-stop) and the camera sets the corresponding shutter speed. Best for landscape photography or any situation that requires depth of field control.
Manual (M)	Photographer sets both aperture and shutter speed. Advanced mode for those with an understanding of photography.
Movie	Camera records short video segments and saves as QuickTime, AVI, or MPEG files. Some models also record sound to accompany the video.
Panorama	Camera designates sequence of shots to be later "stitched together" to create one image with a wide perspective.
Nighttime	Allows for longer shutter speeds, even when the flash is turned on, to enable photography in low ambient light, such as at sunset or for brightly lit interiors. A tripod should be used to help steady the camera when using this mode.

[a] Your camera may have all, some, or only a couple of these modes available. Typically, *Aperture Priority*, *Shutter Priority*, and *Manual* modes are available only on advanced models.

Table A-5. Metering modes with explanation

Metering mode[a]	Explanation
Evaluative Metering	Camera divides viewing area into "segments" and evaluates each area alone and in combination with others. End result is very accurate overall exposure for most scenes. Good choice for general photography.
Spot Metering	Camera only reads center portion of the viewing area, usually within the center brackets or crosshairs. Good choice for situations that require precise exposure control on a particular element in the scene. Most popular use is to correctly meter a person's face in difficult lighting situations.
Center Weighted Metering	Reads entire viewfinder area, but with more emphasis placed on central portion of the scene. Typically used for landscape and general photography. Evaluative metering is usually preferred over center weighted.

[a] Many point-and-shoot cameras only offer one metering mode, usually center weighted or evaluative. Intermediate and advanced models usually include spot metering, too.

Table A-6. Exposure starting points for sunset and astrophotography [a]

Subject	ISO speed	Aperture (f-stop)	Shutter speed
Sunset (point at sky without sun shining in viewfinder)	100	Programmed auto exposure	Programmed auto exposure
Full moon	100	f-8	1/250 to 1/500
Quarter moon	100	f-5.6	1/125 to 1/250
Total lunar eclipse	200	f-2.8	2 seconds (use tripod)
Half lunar eclipse	200	f-4	1 second (use tripod)

Table A-6. Exposure starting points for sunset and astrophotography

Subject	ISO speed	Aperture (f-stop)	Shutter speed
Auroras Borealis	200	f-2.8	2–30 seconds depending on intensity (use tripod)
Star trails	100	f-4	10 minutes or longer (use tripod)
Meteors	100	f-5.6	30 minutes or longer (use tripod)

a The settings in this table should only serve as starting points for astrophotography. Allow ample time for testing with your equipment and conditions for optimum results.

Table A-7. Megapixels to print size reference

Camera type	Photo quality	Acceptable
2MP	5×7	8×10
3MP	8×10	11×14
4MP	11×14	12×16
5MP	12×16	16×20

Table A-8. Number of pictures to capacity of memory card reference a

| Card capacity | Camera resolution | | | | |
	640×480 (.3 MP)	1280×960 (1.3 MP)	1600×1200 (2 MP)	2048×1536 (3.3 MP)	2272×1704 (4.1 MP)
8 MB	29	10	7	3	2
16 MB	58	24	14	8	7
32 MB	120	49	30	17	14
64 MB	241	88	61	35	30
128 MB	483	177	123	71	61

a The number of pictures listed for each memory card size in this chart is for images saved at the highest quality settings. You can "squeeze" more pictures per card by lowering quality settings, but this is not recommended.

Index

We'd like to hear your suggestions for improving our indexes. Send email to
index@oreilly.com.